I SAW IT TOO!

I SAW IT TOO!

Real UFO Sightings

Chris A. Rutkowski

DUNDURN PRESS
TORONTO

Editor: Barry Jowett
Designer: Jennifer Scott
Illustrations: Stacey Archer with Lonigan Gilbert
Printer: Webcom

Library and Archives Canada Cataloguing in Publication

Rutkowski, Chris
    I saw it too! : real UFO sightings / by Chris A. Rutkowski.

ISBN 978-1-55488-448-3

1. Unidentified flying objects--Sightings and encounters--Juvenile literature.   2. Human-alien encounters--Juvenile literature.   I. Title.

TL789.2.R88 2009   j001.942   C2009-903264-3

1   2   3   4   5   13   12   11   10   09

We acknowledge the support of the **Canada Council for the Arts** and the **Ontario Arts Council** for our publishing program. We also acknowledge the financial support of the **Government of Canada** through the **Book Publishing Industry Development Program** and **The Association for the Export of Canadian Books**, and the **Government of Ontario** through the **Ontario Book Publishers Tax Credit program**, and the **Ontario Media Development Corporation.**

Care has been taken to trace the ownership of copyright material used in this book. The author and the publisher welcome any information enabling them to rectify any references or credits in subsequent editions.

J. Kirk Howard, President

Printed and bound in Canada.

www.dundurn.com

Dundurn Press
3 Church Street, Suite 500
Toronto, Ontario, Canada
M5E 1M2

Gazelle Book Services Limited
White Cross Mills
High Town, Lancaster, England
LA1 4XS

Dundurn Press
2250 Military Road
Tonawanda, NY
U.S.A. 14150

CONTENTS

ACKNOWLEDGEMENTS

I would like to thank my family for their patience while I shut myself away in the study many evenings in a row, typing long into the night. I also thank them for inspiring me by giving me dozens and dozens — more like hundreds — of stuffed, plastic, and metal aliens and UFOs that have filled the study and helped me get in the right mood for writing on this subject.

I also need to thank my writers' group, Off The Wall, based in Winnipeg, Canada. Each member of the group has continued to offer me encouragement and suggestions on how to develop and improve my writing. You're a great bunch of gals and guys (and aliens)!

I also need to thank my publisher, The Dundurn Group, for giving me another opportunity to share stories about aliens and UFOs, venturing into young adult literature and creative non-fiction for the first time.

Finally, I must thank my artists, Stacey Archer and Lonigan Gilbert, who spent many long hours drawing, inking, and then doing it all over again to produce a collection of masterpieces!

Oh, and thanks to John Carter of Barsoom.

INTRODUCTION

Every day, no matter where you are or what you are doing, it is likely you will hear something about UFOs or aliens. If you are watching TV, flying saucers or aliens may appear in commercials for pizza or chocolate bars or new cars. Aliens have appeared in episodes of many dramas, cartoons, and comedy shows, not just in science fiction series like *X-Files*, *Star Trek*, and *The Outer Limits*. Of course, UFOs and aliens have appeared in recent movies, too, like *Monsters vs. Aliens*, *Knowing*, and *Indiana Jones and the Kingdom of the Crystal Skull*.

In fact, you may have become so used to seeing UFOs and aliens on television and in movies that you may not be surprised to hear or read about people who say they've really seen them. Quite often there will be stories on the TV news or online news services about UFOs somewhere in the world, some even with video taken with cellphone cameras or surveillance cams. You might not even give these stories more than a quick glance, if at all.

But have you ever wondered, "What would I have done if that was *me* who saw the UFO?" News stories often have experts debating whether the UFOs seen were "real" or simply weather balloons or secret aircraft. But some sightings are by police, airline pilots, or the military. What did they see? Were they simply making their stories up, or was something really there?

Some polls have found that about one in ten people believe they have seen UFOs. If you take the population of your country, your town, your school, or even one of your classes and divide that number by ten, you get a pretty good idea of just how many people have experienced UFO sightings.

Maybe you don't. You may not believe stories about UFOs and aliens, and you might think the people who report seeing them are inventing stories to get attention, or for some other reason. It's easier *not* to believe the stories, because they seem so fantastic.

But what if it happened to you? What if *you* were on a camping trip, walking in a forest one night, and suddenly saw an alien standing next to a UFO? What if *you* were in your bedroom, almost asleep, when a grey-skinned alien appeared and wanted to take you away? What if *you* were playing with friends in a schoolyard one evening after school and a large flying saucer came down from the sky and landed nearby?

Although most UFO sightings are reported by adults, people who investigate UFOs note that the ages of witnesses vary. Some of the most puzzling reports on record during the past sixty years (or longer) of flying saucer and UFO sightings involve kids and teenagers — not just adults with jobs as astronomers, pilots, and police.

What do those kids, teenagers, and young adults actually see? What really happens?

This book is all about UFO sightings and encounters with aliens actually reported by kids and youth your own age. The stories are based on actual UFO investigation files, government records, and newspaper accounts from all around the world.

Did these things really happen? Did the witnesses really see strange flying objects and meet aliens? It's possible they were just mistaken and only thought they saw a flying saucer rather than a car headlight, or an advertising blimp, or a weather balloon, or any one of dozens of other ordinary things seen in odd circumstances.

Is it all true, or just made up? You be the judge.

Just remember: you may see a UFO some day. And if you read about another UFO sighting in the newspaper or watch a TV news story about someone who says she's seen an alien, you might be able to say, "I saw it too!"

ALMOST KIDNAPPED BY A UFO
(Thompson, Canada, 1967)

"**Y**ou can't catch me!" shouted Diana as she ran between the houses.

"Yes I can!" laughed Peter as he gave chase. "You're not 'home free' until you get back to the front steps! I'm going to make you 'it' again!"

"Me too!" yelled Brad. "I'll get you first, you little squirt!"

Her skirt flapping in the breeze, Diana disappeared behind a hedge, giggling, with Peter and Brad in hot pursuit.

The afternoon was hot for Manitoba in June 1967, and it seemed like everyone in the neighbourhood was taking advantage of the good weather by barbecuing for supper. While they did, all the kids were scrambling over and through yards and lanes, chasing one another in sudden games of tag and kick-the-can.

Eight-year-old Diana Lipton and her thirteen-year-old brother Brad had been playing out in their yard with Peter Valentine and his twin sister, Cassie, from across the street. Cassie had become bored of running around in the hot sun and had decided to plop down and rest. Diana and Brad's little sister, Becky, was playing in a sandbox by herself, sitting in the middle of a mound that used to be a carefully made castle.

"No, Becky," sighed Cassie. "Now look what you've done! It took me a whole hour to build that for you and you sat right on top of it!"

Cassie grabbed a shovel out of Becky's hand and began filling a pail again.

"Now, watch how I do this again," she said.

But Becky was offended. She had decided she didn't want any more help, and she shrieked loudly, demanding her shovel back.

"Is everything all right out there?" her mother called, stepping out the back door of their house.

"Yes, Mrs. Lipton," Cassie replied. "We're okay."

"Now, don't get me into any more trouble like last time," she whispered curtly to Becky.

Becky stuck her tongue out and made a triumphant face.

"My shovel!" she said, reaching for it as an angry Cassie looked on.

"I hope none of you kids are fighting or anything," said Bonnie Lipton with her hands planted firmly on her hips. "It's only a half hour or so before our supper and your mother just called, Cassie. Yours is almost ready, and you and Peter will have to be going home soon."

"Yes, Mrs. Lipton," Cassie said, pouting and looking at her feet. As bored as she was, she still didn't want to be going home where there were probably chores waiting.

"My shovel!" Becky said, as if she were trying to get Cassie in trouble on purpose.

Bonnie Lipton looked around the yard, squinting in the bright sun.

"Where are Diana and the boys?" she asked.

Cassie shrugged. "I dunno. They ran off that way," she replied, pointing toward the back of the house.

"Well, you tell them that supper's ready when they come back in the yard," her friends' mother ordered.

Bonnie Lipton went back into the house and started getting plates out of the cupboard. Her husband, Gord, should have been home by now, since he insisted on lighting the barbeque. He claimed he had a "special technique" for getting the coals to just the right temperature and that his burgers tasted so good because of his expertise.

She smiled, thinking of the last time her "expert" barbecued and accidentally singed his favourite fishing hat.

Suddenly, an odd sound filled the room. It seemed to be a slow, beeping noise, starting quietly but gradually getting louder. Puzzled, Bonnie looked around, wondering where it was coming from. Had she left something turned on?

Bonnie went over to the radio, but it was off. She checked in the living room and walked up to the television set, but it was off, too. The sound was still there. She twisted the TV dial and heard the familiar click as it came on. No, that wasn't it.

She wandered throughout the house, but couldn't figure out where the unusual sound was coming from. Then she looked out the kitchen window.

She let out a small gasp, raising a hand to her mouth.

Outside, dirt, leaves and other debris were flying by the window, as if there were a hurricane outside. She turned and looked to a window in a different part of the house and saw that the wind was there, too. The wind was whipping around the house in a counter-clockwise direction.

It's like there's a tornado over our house! she thought to herself. *I'd better get the children inside.*

Running out of the house, Bonnie found herself inside some kind of whirlwind centred on their property. Her hair was blown into her face and dirt stung her eyes. "Becky!" she yelled above the sound of the rushing wind. "Come in right away!"

When they had turned the corner of the house, Peter and Brad had nearly caught Diana in the front yard. She veered suddenly, bared her teeth like a vampire, and raised her hands like claws. "Hisssss!" she pretended, taking them by surprise and forcing Brad to stop and turn so he didn't run into her. But Peter ran headlong into Brad, and the two of them fell into a hedge together.

"Owww!" Peter cried in pain, a bloody scrape starting to appear on his knee.

"Ha!" Diana gloated as she stood on the driveway watching them. "You missed!"

"Why you little —," Brad began, ready to give chase again. But he stopped and looked up into the sky. "Diana, what's that above you?" he said, perplexed.

But she wasn't going to fall for that old trick. "Oh, no you don't, Brad Lipton," she said defiantly. "You're not going to get me *that* way!"

However, as she stood there with the two boys, a strong wind had suddenly started blowing. It seemed to have come from nowhere, but was rushing around them as if a huge fan had been turned on. Diana's hair and clothes started flapping in the strong draft. Dirt blew into her face and she began coughing. She started to turn and run, but found that for some reason her legs didn't want to work.

"Wha … what's happening?" she stammered.

Peter by this time had forgotten about his injury and was watching the scene in front of him with amazement. He stood up, pointing.

"What *is* that thing?" he asked.

Diana was already frightened. Try as she might, she couldn't seem to run away. Panicking, she looked up.

There, not more than twenty feet above her head, was a huge, cube-shaped object, with alternating silver and black sides. Its bottom surface was black, as if she were looking inside a dark box, and the entire thing was slowly rotating counter-clockwise.

It seemed as if the strange object in the sky was somehow causing the wind to blow. Dust, leaves, and old newspapers were being tossed in the air, swirling in a giant circle around them.

Without warning, Diana began to feel as if she was getting lighter and she looked down, shocked to find that her feet were no longer touching the driveway.

"Help!" she screamed as she rose toward the strange cube.

That was enough to spur the boys into action.

"Hey! Let go of her!" Brad shouted. He looked down and found a large rock near the driveway and carefully took aim. He threw it as hard as he could toward the cube, but it had already started to rise and his rock fell short of his target. He found another rock and tried again, with the same result.

By this time Diana was already three feet in the air and her clothes were being pulled up on her body as if she were being sucked up into a vacuum cleaner.

"I'll get her!" Peter said as he ran toward her. In his best imitation of a defensive end on a football team, he launched himself into the air and tackled Diana around her knees. He held on tight and felt a strong tug that pulled him up, then suddenly released them both. They fell, sprawling onto the grass.

Mr. Gord Lipton was nearly home, driving along his street, when he noticed that the wind had picked up considerably.

"That's funny," he said aloud. "The weather forecast said it was going to be calm and clear today."

When he pulled into his driveway, he saw Peter, the neighbours' boy from across the street, lying on top of Diana in the yard. Then he saw Brad jump on top of the two of them.

He stopped the car and rolled down the window. Dirt and leaves blew into the car as he poked his head out. "What's going on?" he demanded.

In answer, Brad pointed into the sky. "It's that thing," he said, trembling. "It was going to take her!"

As Gord Lipton opened the car door, a shout made him turn and look away.

"What's happening?" asked Cassie, with Becky in tow. "We heard Diana screaming."

"That thing was sucking her up into the air," Peter offered, shaking and still in shock.

Gord Lipton noted the two boys were ghostly white, trembling, and very scared. Something odd obviously had occurred.

He turned his gaze upward and saw a peculiar, boxlike object hanging in the air. It was moving slowly away from them, but it was close enough that he could see that it looked hollow on the bottom. It certainly didn't look like any aircraft or helicopter he had ever seen. As impossible as it seemed, the strange object appeared to be the cause of the dust and debris flying all around. As it flew further away, the wind died down.

"What the heck was that?" he wondered aloud.

He then ran over to Diana as the boys stood up. Diana was limp and looked like she was asleep.

"Diana," her father pleaded. "Say something. Are you all right?"

Dazed, Diana blinked her eyes and moaned softly. "What's going on?" she asked after a few moments, looking at the small crowd that had gathered around her. "Why am I on the ground? Did Peter catch me? Am I 'it'?"

By this time, Bonnie Lipton had run out from around the side of her house.

"Becky! Diana! I was calling for you! Are you all right?" she exclaimed, nearly out of breath. She looked down at Diana. "I was worried you were all outside in that wind," she said with concern in her voice.

"What wind?" asked little Becky.

Sure enough, as the object rose higher into the sky, the wind died down and the air was once again still and silent. The strange craft was now tilted at a forty-five-degree angle and was flying away over the trees and neighbouring houses. As they all watched, it moved soundlessly away and eventually disappeared in the distance.

"Diana, what was it like being in the air like that?" asked her brother.

Still a bit dazed, Diana frowned and looked at him, glassy-eyed. "What do you mean?" she replied. "You were chasing me, and then I think I fell."

Brad's eyes widened. "Don't you remember being sucked up into the air?" he asked, incredulous. "Peter had to grab you and pull you back down!"

Horrified, Diana shook her head. "No, all I know is that it suddenly got very windy," she said. "But ... how did everyone get here? I don't remember Dad getting home."

Her father walked away, then called to them. "Look at this," he said. He pointed to the ground near the house as they walked over. "There's a big circular area of dirt and leaves around our house, but nothing on anyone else's yard. And I just raked yesterday."

"It's like a big dome of some sort was over top of us," said his wife, puzzled. "And we were inside a Christmas snow globe, but with leaves instead of snow!"

Throughout the rest of the afternoon, they checked with other neighbours and found no one else had seen or heard the whirlwind. No one had seen the cube. And no one else had seen Diana's levitation.

Mr. Lipton had made many calls to the police, the weather office, and the local newspaper. The airport had no record of any aircraft being in the area that afternoon and no other unusual objects had been reported. Eventually, UFO investigators heard about the incident and visited the Liptons. They spoke at length with the children and their parents, then spent some time looking around the yard. They told the Liptons they could not find any explanation for the case.

Only Brad and Peter had actually seen Diana almost kidnapped by a UFO.

Source: Chris Rutkowski, *Unnatural History: True Manitoba Mysteries* (Winnipeg, MB: Chameleon Publishers, 1993), 26–28.

Questions a Ufologist Would Ask:

1. What do you think happened to Diana? Was she really sucked up into the air by a strange flying object?

2. If it was a craft from another planet, do you think aliens would want to snatch us away with a "levitation" device? Are there other ways they could take us on board?

ATTACKED BY ALIENS
(Chico, Venezuela, 1954)

It was almost dark, but Lorenzo Flores and Jesus Gomez were determined to shoot a rabbit that night. They had been out hunting all afternoon and were hot and tired from climbing across the rocky outcrops of the *paramos*, the swampy highlands along the Andes Mountains in southern Venezuela, in December 1954.

The sun had set a short time earlier, but the two boys still thought they could catch something before it got too late, even if it was only a small ground squirrel.

That afternoon they had walked out of their tiny village near the town of Chico and followed the Trans-Andean Highway for a few miles until they decided they were in a good hunting spot. Then they marked their entry point carefully before heading into the bush.

Now, they were nearing the highway again as they retraced their trail. Both were good trackers and knew they value of safety in the wilderness. Only once had they become lost and that was a long time ago, before they had learned to take more care and blaze their trail carefully.

Jesus, with his rifle slung on his back, was in the lead now, as he usually was, always wanting to be the first in everything. He

was also the older of the two, having just turned sixteen. His tall frame allowed him to take bigger strides and maybe that's why his companion seemed to fall behind so much.

But Lorenzo, although a year younger, was easily a match for Jesus's speed. He was nearly a foot shorter, but was extremely agile and nimble and able to dart among the rocks and spiny cacti with ease.

Jesus stopped when he reached the highway and sat down on a flat rock beside the road.

"Come on," he shouted to Lorenzo. "I think there's a truck coming. Maybe we can get a ride back home."

Lorenzo walked into sight and looked down the road.

"Oh, are you too weak to walk?" he jibed. "You should have eaten more lunch today!"

Jesus grinned and said, "No, I'm fine. I was worrying more about you having to carry your rifle much longer!"

He ducked when Lorenzo kicked some dirt at him. Jesus knew Lorenzo was very proud of his new rifle. He had just bought it with money he had earned by selling birds and monkeys to pet-store buyers from America. It had taken him a year to get the amount the *cantina* manager wanted for the gun. He did not have a sling for it, but carried it carefully, only occasionally letting it out of his grasp when resting it gently against a tree.

"So, where is this truck?" Lorenzo asked impatiently. He was unhappy about not catching a rabbit that day and wanted nothing more than to go home to bed.

Jesus looked down the road to where he thought he had seen a set of headlights. "That's funny," he said. "I was sure there was something on the road there." He squinted, but could not see any light on the roadway. There was another light, just off to the side, not far off the highway. "There. What's that?"

Lorenzo looked to where Jesus was pointing, a light that seemed to be in some low trees not far away. The yellow glow seemed to be getting brighter and was shimmering, as if it were under water. "Come on!" he shouted excitedly. "Maybe a truck ran off the road and the people need help!" He grabbed his rifle and started running down the road, this time in the lead.

Jesus ran after him, finding some new energy through his excitement. He remembered two years ago a bus had turned over near there and many people were hurt in the accident.

The boys almost flew down the dirt road, following its snaking path over gently rolling hills until they reached a point that was nearest to the light.

"Look here," Lorenzo said. "There are no tire tracks or any sign that something drove off the road into the trees."

Jesus agreed. "But what else could the light be? No one lives near here."

"Perhaps a night spirit," Lorenzo replied with a big grin. "Your mother is always talking about such things!"

Jesus laughed, but then became serious. "Maybe an airplane crashed. Let's find it, then we can go for help."

"Good idea."

The two walked into the brush and started weaving their way toward the source of the light. After only a few minutes, they came upon a clearing. They froze in total shock at what they saw.

There, before them, was a shiny, metallic object that looked like two soup bowls joined rim to rim. It was as large as a car and seemed to be hovering about three feet above the ground. The strange thing was glowing and there was an orange flame coming from somewhere underneath it.

"What is this thing?" whispered Lorenzo, very scared.

Jesus could barely answer. "I don't know! I've never seen any pictures of airplanes that look like this!"

They both stood watching the object, unable to move because of their fear. Suddenly, things got much worse.

Four small creatures came out from behind the craft and started coming toward them. The beings looked like small men, but were only about three feet tall and were covered with long, dark hair. Their eyes were huge, round discs that looked the size of saucers and they stared at the boys in a way that made the pair shake with fear.

The creatures had long, thin arms, and their hands had four fingers with long, sharp claws, like a hawk. As they came toward the boys, the monsters reached out to them with their talons.

Although frightened, Jesus and Lorenzo snapped out of their frozen panic, realizing they were in danger.

"Run!" screamed Lorenzo.

They both turned and started scrambling back the way they had come.

Lorenzo ran quickly between some shrubs and rocks and was making some headway when he heard a cry behind him. He looked back just in time to see Jesus stumble and fall.

"Jesus!" he shouted. "Get up! They're right behind you!"

He watched helplessly as Jesus tried to regain his footing, but it was too late. The creatures reached Jesus and bent over him.

"*Aiieeee!*" Jesus cried when the beings stretched their arms toward him.

Lorenzo sprang into action to save his friend. He ran back to where the creatures had Jesus pinned on the ground. Even though they were small, they appeared to have great strength. The five of them were too much for Jesus to handle.

One of the beings had Jesus in a headlock while the other four were trying to hold on to his legs and arms. Jesus was putting up a good fight, flailing his limbs and managing to get some good kicks in.

The creature that had its arms around Jesus's head was making some low, snarling sounds. Its mouth was open slightly and Lorenzo could see some sharp teeth inside.

"Get away from him!" Lorenzo shouted angrily as he reached them. "Let my friend go!"

He grabbed the arm of the one nearest him. Its hairy body was well-muscled despite its size, and it fought Lorenzo off easily. It pushed him away with a strength Lorenzo had never seen before.

The other beings did not take any notice of him, but continued attacking his friend. One had a firm grip on Jesus's leg now, and they all started dragging the struggling boy toward the strange craft.

Looking around on the ground for something to hit them with, Lorenzo realized his rifle was not far away, where he had dropped it among some small shrubs. He ran to where it lay and picked it up quickly.

Lorenzo held up the rifle. He realized it was not loaded and that by the time he was able to get ammunition into the chambers it might be too late, but he could still use it as a weapon!

He moved behind the creature that had Jesus's head and raised his gun in the air, holding it by the muzzle. The hairy dwarf took no notice of him. Lorenzo brought the rifle down hard on the monster's head.

The rifle broke in two, as if it had struck a rock. The creature let out a loud yelp and let go of Jesus, who slumped to the ground. The others stopped trying to pull Jesus with them and also let him alone. They all turned to look at Lorenzo, who had a desperate expression on his face and was brandishing what was left of his gun.

"Get away, I said!" ordered Lorenzo with lots of machismo and renewed confidence. "I'll take you all on!"

The creatures seemed to confer with each other, soundlessly, and then started running back through the bush to the craft.

Lorenzo didn't bother to wonder why they did that, but bent over Jesus, who was now unconscious. He slapped his face gently, saying, "Jesus! Jesus!"

Jesus started moaning and moving his head from side to side. He was scratched on his face and arms and his shirt was ripped and torn in several places. Lorenzo looked down at his own clothes and saw that his shirt, too, had been torn by the creatures' claws.

He heard a loud roaring sound and looked up to see the strange craft rise into the air. It paused for a moment, glowed a brilliant white, then zipped away across the hills, almost too fast to follow. In a few seconds, it was gone, leaving the boys alone in the bush, with only the sounds of the night to keep them company.

"I'd say you had a run-in with a wild boar," said Dr. Mendez after dressing Lorenzo's bandages.

After Jesus had recovered enough to walk, he and Lorenzo had slowly trekked back to their village, where their worried parents were waiting for them.

Upon seeing their condition and hearing their bizarre tale, the local doctor was called.

"But Papa," Lorenzo insisted. "It did happen! Those creatures attacked us and were going to take Jesus with them!"

His father frowned and turned to Jesus, whose own family was in the same room. Since the boys returned, they had been hysterical as they told their families a wild story about flying ships and little monsters. It was all he and their mother could do to calm them down, and Jesus's parents were just as puzzled by their son's behaviour. Neither boy had ever acted this way before, or made up tall tales.

"Is this true?" he asked the boy. "Were there really any small little men?"

Jesus had many bruises and blood had oozed from several deep gouges on his arms and legs. He was no longer dazed, and was adamant that his experience had been real. "Yes!" he said firmly. "I was fighting with them, but then I must have blacked out. I don't remember how they left. I was sure I was going to be taken by them."

"My friend saved my life," he added, grinning at Lorenzo.

"Ridiculous!" the doctor snorted. "You two are lying! There are no such things as hairy dwarves or flying craft like you described."

"We'll prove it!" Jesus shouted. "We'll take you there and show you."

"Yes, right now," Lorenzo chimed in.

Lorenzo's father thought for a minute then turned to the other boy's father. "What do you say, Hector?" he asked. "Shall we go now?"

Hector Gomez nodded immediately. "Yes, but only if the doctor goes with us, too."

Mendez stood up. "All right," he exclaimed. "If only to prove there is nothing to this foolishness." He added, "But let's get the police sergeant to come with us, too."

"Yes, good idea," said Lorenzo. "He can protect us if they come back."

Dr. Mendez was startled by the boy's remark. He was certain that threatening to bring the police along would make the boys change their story and own up to the truth.

A small army of people from the village went out to the spot that night. All were able to see crushed grass and disturbed dirt where there obviously had been a struggle of some sort. There were even long gouges in the earth that might have been made by the heels of a young boy's shoes as he was dragged along the ground.

What's more, they found pieces of Lorenzo's gun. The wood had shattered from some impact and the metal was bent.

However, there was no sign of the creatures or the unusual flying craft.

"I don't know what to think of this," said Hector Gomez to Lorenzo's father when the group had returned to the village. The men were sitting in the kitchen, talking about the incident. "Why would they make up such a story?"

"I don't know," was the reply. "Lorenzo has never been this upset before. And how do you explain their injuries?"

Dr. Mendez coughed. "I still say they made it all up," he said. "But ..." he paused before finishing. "There *is* one thing that bothers me."

"What is that?" Hector asked.

The doctor thought for a minute before answering. "Did you not say Lorenzo had saved all his money to buy that rifle?" he finally asked. "Was it not his most valued possession?"

"Yes, it was."

"Then why would he deliberately break it just to support a tall tale?" Mendez wondered.

Source: Coral and Jim Lorenzen, *Encounters with UFO Occupants* (New York: Berkeley Publishing, 1976), 145–146.

Questions a Ufologist Would Ask:

1. If Jesus was not attacked by aliens, how do you think he got the cuts and bruises on his body?

2. According to some writers about UFOs, aliens want to abduct people aboard their space ships for examination and other studies of our bodies. What do you think the aliens wanted to do with Jesus? Why did they stop and go away when Lorenzo threatened them with his rifle?

THE FLATWOODS MONSTER
(West Virginia, USA, 1952)

"**G**o out for a long one!" Neil said as he faded back.

Sean leapt off his mark and ran downfield. He zigzagged to avoid Will, who was doing his best to block his path.

The three boys loved football and enjoyed playing quick games of pass-and-run whenever they could. It was early evening on September 12, 1952, and the school year had barely begun, yet everyone seemed to have "football fever" in the entire state of West Virginia. Here in the small town of Flatwoods, the football field was always being used by groups of teenagers imitating their favourite college quarterbacks and halfbacks.

"You won't get past me!" Will shouted, panting, as he veered in front of Sean.

Sean bumped roughly into him and looked over his shoulder for the football Neil had already launched in his direction.

"Ooof!" he gasped as Will got in a good block. He was slowed down just enough that when he reached for the ball, it sailed over the tips of his fingers.

Sean fell to the field on top of Will, who was grinning from ear to ear.

"Gotcha!" Will said.

"Awww! You haven't caught one today!" Neil shouted from downfield.

"Well, if we were playing a real game, Will would have had a penalty for pass interference!" Sean said.

But Will ignored him. "It's my turn now! You go out for a pass!"

Before they could start another play, however, Neil called out to them. He was standing and looking up into the sky, staring at something in their direction but above their heads. He pointed behind them toward the end zone. "Look at that!" he said. "It's a plane on fire!"

The other boys turned to look up in the sky. There, flying low over some trees, was a slow-moving red ball of light. It sailed along the horizon, making no sound but appearing to be a large aircraft of some sort, even though it didn't have the usual lights of an airplane. Since it was already 7:15 p.m. and starting to get dark, the plane should have had some running lights or wingtip lights visible, but there were none to be seen.

While they watched, the bright object suddenly stopped and seemed to hover over a hill not more than half a mile away.

"That's not a plane!" Will said excitedly.

"Nope, that sure doesn't look like a plane," said Sean. "Maybe it's a helicopter from the army base."

Then, as they watched, the object dropped behind the hill and a bright orange glow grew from where it went down, as though there had been an explosion.

"Wow!" said Sean. "It crashed! Let's go look!"

"Yeah!" Neil said when he ran up to them. "Maybe it's a meteorite or something!"

"Or maybe a flying saucer!" Will laughed.

The three teenagers ran across the field and headed out of the park. As they ran, they passed the house of some friends who were out in their yard.

"Hi, Neil!" called Joel May, practising tennis with his brother Adam. "Where're you all going?"

The trio paused only briefly in their quest.

"Didn't you see it?" asked Sean. "The thing that crashed over that hill?"

Adam shook his head. "No, we were chasing Sheba. That darn dog grabbed our tennis ball and took off."

The German shepherd bounded up to them, right on cue. She dropped the ball at their feet and barked playfully, wanting some more fun.

"We saw a bright light go down behind the hill," explained Will. "Look, there's still a glow there now."

Sure enough, when they all looked to the horizon, there was a red glow pulsing from behind the trees.

"What's all the excitement about out here?" said Joel and Adam's mom, joining them. She was babysitting another neighbour's child, little Tommy Hyer, and had just come outside with him.

Adam turned to his mother and asked, "Mom, can I go with Will and the others looking for the thing that crashed?"

"What are you talking about?" Kathleen May replied.

The boys related what they had seen and pointed to the red glow among the trees not far off. As they talked, another boy, seventeen-year-old Gene Lemon, came by on his bicycle.

"Did you see the light in the sky?" he asked. "I'm going to find out what it was. There was a bright thing that was in the sky and then dropped right down behind the hill. I think it might have been an army plane that crashed. I brought a flashlight to help light the way."

Joel pleaded with their mother. "*Pleeeease* can we go?"

Kathleen May had her hands full with Tommy and was flustered. "Yes — I mean, no! Oh, I'll go with you! We'll all go looking for this thing. But we can't stay long. It's already getting dark. And I have to put Tommy to bed soon."

"Yay!" shouted Adam. "Let's go!"

The group set out together through the meadows and treed lots on a winding trail. They could still see the glow ahead and, as they got closer, it seemed to get brighter.

"Sure doesn't look like a plane crashed," said Neil, in the lead.

Sheba had run ahead of them all, barking joyfully. They could hear her crashing through the bush down the path in front of them, heading for the light.

But suddenly, that changed. They heard her bark furiously then let out a sharp yelp. Soon, she ran back from the light, her tail between her legs. She shot past them, heading for home.

"Dear me!" said Mrs. May. "Sheba's never acted like that before. She's not afraid of anything. I wonder what happened."

It had become noticeably eerier since they started out. The sky was darkening quickly and a light breeze was blowing through the trees. They all started shivering, probably because of the cooling of the night, although there was something about the situation that was making them uneasy.

"I'm scared," sobbed Tommy, missing his mother and father. "I want to go home!"

Concerned now, Kathleen May picked up Tommy and held him tightly. "It's okay," she reassured him. "We'll be back home soon." She was about to head back when she noticed that a strange mist had appeared on the ground, covering their feet.

"What's that smell?" asked Neil.

Gene wrinkled his nose in disgust. "Yeah! P-U!"

"My eyes hurt!" said Adam. "It's this fog, I think."

"What is it?" asked Mrs. May. "It's not like regular marsh gas. It's different."

"Look there!" Gene shouted as they rounded a hill. There in front of them was a large ball of fire, only about fifty feet away, just sitting on the ground.

"It's as big as a house!" gasped Mrs. May.

Behind them, others in the group had not made it to the hill yet, and hadn't seen the ball of fire, but Mrs. May heard a cry behind her. When she turned to look at them, she became even more concerned.

Will and Sean had stopped and were still twenty or thirty feet back down the trail. They stood, staring up into a tree along the path.

"Th-there!" Sean said, trembling and pointing with a shaky hand. "In the trees!"

Mrs. May ran back to them with Tommy in her arms. When she looked over to the oak tree, she saw two small lights halfway up in the branches.

Gene came up to join them.

"Oh, it's probably just an owl or raccoon," he said. "Here, I'll shine my flashlight on it."

He raised the beam and they got the shock of their lives.

There in the air was a giant creature wearing a helmet of some sort, through which they could clearly see two blue "eyes" shining out. The rest of the face or head was enveloped in blackness. The creature's head, with the helmet on it, looked like it was an ace of spades. Its arms were not in sight, but its huge body looked like that of a large, stocky man, and it hovered in the trees about six feet above the ground.

Tommy began crying and buried his face in Kathleen's shoulder. "I want my mommy!" he squeaked, frightened out of his wits.

"Good gosh!" Mrs. May whispered, very afraid and wondering how she was going to get all the children safely home.

"It's coming toward us!" shouted Neil as he hid beside a cluster of saplings.

The monster began gliding slowly in their direction, its eyes focused steadily beyond them, as if looking for something. It circled nearer to them, and they could see it better until the flashlight beam went out when Gene fell backward, fainting dead away.

But instead of attacking, the strange being flew over them, heading for the fiery object around the hill further up the path.

"Let's get out of here!" screamed Mrs. May when the creature had passed. "Come on! All of you!"

She began rounding up the troop and steering them down the path toward home.

"What about Gene?" Will asked. "He's asleep or something!"

Mrs. May thought for a moment. Then she gave him Tommy to hold. "Here," she said. "You take Tommy and go home with Joel and Adam. Neil and Sean, you help me carry Gene."

The two boys each grabbed a leg and she held his arms. They managed to make it almost all the way down the path before having to set him down to rest. Fortunately, he was starting to wake up and was able to stand on his own.

The others were already waiting for them at the house. Their eyes were still watering from the foul-smelling mist. Joel was coughing a lot and Tommy was crying steadily, beside himself with fear. Mrs. May went to comfort him and take him back to his own family. On the way, she called a neighbour, who came running over to help calm everyone. Every one of the boys was practically hysterical with fear; they were shaking and pale, and babbling about the monster.

It was going to be a long night.

"So, tell me again about the flying monster," Lee Stewart asked Gene. The editor of the local newspaper, he had heard about the incident from Kathleen May's neighbour, who had bandaged some of Gene's scratches while people gathered at the house once word had spread. Stewart had persuaded Gene to lead him back to the site of the encounter that night with strong flashlights.

"I told you," Gene said wearily as they trudged along the path. "It had a diving helmet of some kind, with a round, clear part that its eyes shone through. It gave me the chills and I felt hypnotized. Then it came right over me as it went back to its ship. I must have blacked out."

They played their beams on the ground and trees ahead. When they reached the spot where the encounter took place they found that the ball of fire and the giant creature were nowhere to be seen.

"It's gone now," Gene said. "But this is where it happened."

The newspaper man walked around the clearing. "Hmmm," he thought out loud. "I wonder what it could have been."

He bent down to look at the grass. "Phew!" he said in disgust. "Something here smells terrible." He coughed and sneezed once, then twice. "Okay, I've seen enough for tonight. Let's get you home to bed."

Early the next morning, Lee Stewart went back to the spot to see what it looked like in bright daylight. Around the area, he found what he thought were skid marks about ten feet apart. The marks came down the hill from the tree where the monster had first been seen, all the way to where the strange craft had been sitting. There, a wide patch of the tall grass was crushed flat, as if by a heavy weight. But the soft ground underneath it was not pressed down at all. It looked like a large object moved or was dragged down the hill, affecting the grass but not the soil underneath it.

Making inquiries, Stewart had found out that about the same time as the group had met the monster in the trees, a man living about ten miles away had called the local sheriff's office about a bright, flaming object he had seen crash into a nearby hill. The sheriff was actually investigating the report when the call came in about Mrs. May and the others.

Stewart was most impressed with the fact that they were all very upset and visibly frightened by what they had seen. In fact, they all told such similar stories, it was hard to imagine that they would try to make it all up. They certainly weren't trying to sell their story to the newspaper or a magazine, so why would they make up such a thing? He thought it was possible that the red-eyed monster gliding over them might have been an owl that looked weird because of the way the flashlight beam hit it, but they were all sure it had not been an owl or any other bird.

"Was it a monster or robot going back to its flying saucer?" the newspaper story he wrote asked. "What would have made the boys and Mrs. May so terrified? None of them had ever told a tall tale before, so is it possible they really saw the Flatwoods Monster?"

Source: Jerome Clark, *The UFO Encyclopedia, Volume 2: The Emergence of a Phenomenon: UFOs from the Beginning through 1959* (Detroit, MI: Omnigraphics, 1992), 144–146.

Questions a Ufologist Would Ask:

1. Not all UFOs remain unexplained. Some turn out to have
    explanations and are actually natural or manmade things seen
    from odd angles or under unusual conditions. A bright object
    seen falling to the ground is sometimes explained as a meteor,
    fireball, or what astronomers call a *bolide*.

    Sometimes, bolides are described as looking like "air-
    planes on fire" and speeding across the sky toward the ground.
    They are often thought to be falling close by, "just over the
    next hill" or "in the field across the highway," but are really
    many miles away and only look nearby because they are so
    bright and large. Have you ever seen one of these? What did
    it look like to you?

THE SHEPHERD
(Villares del Saz, Spain, 1953)

The newspaper editor wiped his brow and stared at the young teenager sitting anxiously across from him. *Is this boy telling the truth about what happened?* he wondered to himself.

"You know that such things do not exist," he stated, as if commanding Máximo to agree. There had been many stories in the newspapers about flying saucers seen by people around the world, especially *Americanos*, but some people in Europe had seen them, too. In fact, some people in their own district had said they had seen unusual objects flying in the sky, but he wanted this boy to tell his story and see if it matched what had already been reported.

Máximo Hernáiz was fourteen years old. He had been raised by his parents to always tell the truth — no matter what — so he bravely answered the man glaring at him across the worn wooden desk.

"But *Señor*," he said, "I did see the *globo grande*! It was there!"

"Very well," the man said. "Tell me again what happened. When did you go to the field?"

Máximo started from the beginning, for the third time. He said, "It was about ten o'clock, by the sun ..."

The morning was already hot and stifling, and Máximo was obediently finishing his household chores after breakfast, although much slower than usual.

"Máximo," his mother told him, "you are as slow as a caterpillar today. Did you not get a good sleep last night?"

"Oh, no, mother." He laughed. "It is such a nice morning, I am enjoying the day. Maybe if I go slow, the day will last longer!"

His mother rolled her eyes and shook her head. *What a silly boy!* she thought to herself.

Máximo finally left the house and went into the fields to mind the cattle. It was his job, as cowherd, to make sure the animals were fed but that they stayed away from the crops. He did not go to school, as he had to help his parents on their farm near the village of Villares del Saz, east of Madrid in central Spain.

Máximo did not own a watch, so he had to rely on his own instinct and his careful observation of the sun to calculate time. This was something that you didn't learn in school; it was knowledge that you gained from working and living on the land.

He looked at the blinding, hot ball in the sky and knew it was still some ways away from its highest point in its movement, arching across the heavens. He would have a few hours before he could eat the fresh bread and olives his mother had packed him for lunch in his shoulder bag.

He playfully chased the cows into the far part of the pasture, with one of their friendly farm dogs at his side. The countryside was gently rolling, with trees scattered throughout the area. Máximo thought this was the most beautiful place in the whole world.

After a while, he looked to where the sun was again and saw

that it was reaching its highest point in the sky. It was noon, and time to eat lunch.

Máximo sat on the side of a small hill along the side of the field and watched the cattle. Although it was a boring job, it was good to be out in the sun and fresh air.

It was sometime after noon, perhaps one o'clock, that he heard a faint whistling sound that he thought was another farm-hand some distance away. A boy about his age, named Marcus, often brought his family's cattle near the fence on the side of their property, and the two of them occasionally could sit together for a short while. Máximo didn't turn around to look until he heard the sound again, fading in and out, and this time it seemed closer.

He looked over his shoulder and was shocked to see a bright object like a large balloon — *un globo grande* — like those that he had sometimes seen at country fairs. But as he turned and stood up to get a better look, he realized this was not a balloon, but something much stranger.

The unusual object was glowing very brightly, like the sun, but its yellow colour was more like some electric farm lights that he could see at night down the dirt tracks toward town. This object was only a bit bigger than the balloons at fairs — about four or five feet wide — and was shaped like the round water jug that he used when he carried water from the well to his home. It seemed to be settling onto the field not far from him. Its glow was fading and he could see it was now taking on a metallic grey colour, like tin.

He watched it for a short time, wondering what this odd thing could be. Then he decided that it might be a balloon after all and started walking toward it. But before he reached it, a hatch or door opened on top and something came out.

Máximo was astonished by what he saw: three little "men" climbed out from inside the odd vehicle.

"Oh, little *tietes*!" he exclaimed, thinking they looked like tiny versions of people, and calling them the name he used for friendly villagers. Each of these little creatures was less than two feet high and squat in shape, like chubby versions of dolls that Máximo's sister played with.

They were wearing smart-looking blue suits that were tight to their bodies, much like musicians or dancers Máximo had seen sometimes at the fair. On their heads were little flat, peaked caps and they had what looked like metal sheets on their arms. The little men had narrow, slanted eyes set in yellow-coloured faces that Máximo thought made them look, as he described it, "Oriental."

All three jumped down from the top of their craft and walked quickly up to Máximo. One stood on either side of him and one directly in front of him. This one began speaking in an odd language to him, but Máximo didn't understand. He shook his head rapidly, but the little fellow didn't like that very much. He seemed to get angry, perhaps because he wasn't being understood, and he suddenly slapped Máximo in the face. Máximo was startled; he didn't know how to react.

As they stared at one another, the three men must have decided that Máximo was not the person they wanted to deal with, because they turned and walked back to their round vehicle. They reached up to some kind of rung or bar attached to the craft and used it to pull themselves up to the top.

As Máximo continued to watch in amazement, the door on top swung shut and the object began to glow again. It brightened until it was again like the sun and rose up into the air quickly. Máximo could follow it with his eyes for a short time before it was lost in the distance.

After the bright globe had left, Máximo began shaking and, even though he tried, he could not seem to stop. Not knowing what to do, he found himself suddenly running home to tell his parents what had happened. The cows chased after him, puzzled as to why it was time to go home so soon.

His mother and father were surprised he had come back and scolded him for bringing the cows home early.

"Máximo," his mother said to him, "you know better than to cut short the cows' pasture time. It will upset their schedule, and we will not get as much milk today!"

"I'm sorry, Mama," he answered, "but I was frightened by the *tietes* that came out of the ball of light."

"What nonsense is this?" his father asked. "Were the villagers playing tricks on you?"

"No, Papa," Máximo replied. "I do not know who they were. They were very strange, and only as big as Luisa's dolls."

As she listened, Máximo's mother realized that her son was pale and shaking.

"Máximo," she asked with concern. "Are you all right?" She felt his cheek and found it to be cold and damp. "Sit down," she told him.

"I am good," he said, although he wasn't sure that he believed it himself.

"What happened in the pasture?" his father wanted to know.

Máximo explained what had happened, but of course his parents at first did not believe their son's fanciful story. But when he insisted it was true, they didn't know what to believe.

His father eventually decided that his son must have been telling the truth. After all, what reason would he have to make up such a story? He contacted the local police station and an officer soon came to their house, thinking that perhaps Máximo had seen an aircraft accident.

After hearing his story, the policeman wanted to see the place where the globe had landed, so Máximo led him and his father back to the spot where he had seen the balloon-shaped craft. There, in the soft ground of the pasture, were tiny footprints and several holes two inches deep and an inch across, arranged in a perfect square one foot on each side. There was no question that something had happened there. But what?

"What, indeed?" harrumphed the newspaper editor. He knew that he had received many reports from people throughout the area who had reported seeing similar odd, flying objects.

He had even interviewed a police officer from Honrubia, not far from Villares, who told him, "We saw a grey ball hanging silently in the sky, and as we watched it suddenly flew quickly off to the east, as if it had come from the Villares area."

The editor looked patiently at the boy sitting in front of him. He held up the newspaper that had just been printed that day, July 12, 1953.

"Máximo," he finally said, "can you tell me what this headline says?"

The boy looked at the paper and frowned. Then he lowered his chin.

"I am sorry, *señor*, I cannot. I cannot read," he said, a bit embarrassed.

"Have you heard stories of 'little green men'?" asked the editor.

The boy looked up, excitedly. "No, *señor*. The men I saw were dressed all in blue!"

The newspaperman sighed. How could an illiterate cowherder have made up such a wild tale if he didn't know how to read stories about flying saucers that were being reported in newspapers around the world?

Máximo left the newspaper office for the long walk back to

his farm with his father. He knew that the little men really existed, and that he had not been sleeping while watching the cows, as that would have been a terrible mistake. But if the adults were telling him that it couldn't have happened, what did he see?

Source: Charles Bowen, ed., *The Humanoids* (London: Futura, 1974), 77–83.

Questions a Ufologist Would Ask:

1. If there are aliens on other planets, it is reasonable to assume they must communicate with one another in some kind of language. It is interesting to "make up" another language as a way of understanding our own language, whether it's English, French, Spanish, or Chinese. On TV and in movies, writers have made up languages such as Klingon, Romulan, and Ewok. Try making up your own language and share it with a few friends as a secret way of communicating. "Hello" could be "zorg," for example. "I" could be "Jee," "you" could be "tux," "play" could be "lopo," and "game" could be "eks-boks." So, if you want to ask a friend to play a video game with you, you could say: "Tux lopo eks-boks jee?"

2. What do you think the "little man" was trying to say to Máximo?

3. If you were trying to communicate with someone who didn't know your language, how could you make yourself understood?

"YODA"
(Ottawa, Canada, 1995)

Although **many governments around the** world insist they are not "officially" interested in UFOs, many have admitted that they have been keeping files on UFO reports. In fact, during the past several years, some countries have released official documents about UFO sightings reported by their own citizens.

In England, the Ministry of Defence has been making public thousands of pages of memos and letters from people who have reported seeing UFOs. Many of the reports have even been from police and members of the British Army and Royal Air Force who saw strange flashing lights or metallic discs darting about the sky and made official reports to their superiors.

In the United States, the air force operated several secret projects devoted to keeping track of UFO reports. One of these was called Project Blue Book, which eventually listed more than thirteen thousand separate UFO reports before being shut down in 1969. All of these reports have been released to the public, and the enormous number of cases proves that many, many people saw unusual objects in the American skies.

Even governments of countries that have been closed to the West have released some studies of UFO reports. The Soviet Union (now broken up into many separate countries, such as Russia and Kazakhstan) allowed some documents about studies of UFO reports to be made available as well.

Some European countries, such as France, Italy, and Spain, have given UFO researchers access to UFO files. France even had an official science department devoted to recording and investigating UFOs seen there.

Because it borders the United States, Canada has shared some official investigations of UFOs with American projects and studies. There were two Canadian military studies of UFOs: Project Magnet and Project Second Story, both of which were closed long ago. UFO reports investigated by these official studies have been made available publicly as well. Since then, other groups not part of the military or government have been involved in recording UFO sightings. One of these is Ufology Research, which in 2008 alone studied more than one thousand UFO reports in Canada.

Many Canadian UFO sightings were reported to its air force, but also to the Royal Canadian Mounted Police (RCMP), which then passed information on to other agencies. These cases are now part of the public record, and some of them are fantastic in their detail and description. Some involved teenagers and young adults as witnesses, and one Canadian case in particular stands out because it is so unusual.

It was late in the afternoon of March 19, 1995, when Major Jacques Gendreau of the National Defence Centre in Ottawa, Canada, received a phone call. It was his job to receive calls from people who wanted to report their sightings of UFOs to the air force.

Usually, Major Gendreau got calls from people who had seen stars, planets, or meteors and mistakenly thought they were spacecraft from other planets. Sometimes people saw airplanes or helicopters far away or at low angles so that lights on their wings or passenger compartments looked very strange. Most of the time, Major Gendreau was able to reassure callers that what they had experienced were simple mistakes of observation. Of course, some people refused to believe his explanations and thought that the military or government was involved in a "cover-up" of secret UFO information.

It was just after 4:30 p.m. on this particular day when the phone rang and Major Gendreau picked it up.

"Hello, National Defence," he said, thinking that perhaps this would be the last call of the day before his shift was over and he could go home for supper.

"Is this where I can report an encounter with aliens?" a woman's voice asked.

The officer sighed and groaned inwardly. Was this another prank call by a teenager?

"How can I help you, ma'am?" he answered patiently.

"It's my son," she said. "I think that aliens abducted him."

"Abducted?" the major asked. "You mean he was kidnapped?"

There was a pause at the other end of the line. "I ... I'm not sure, exactly," the woman slowly said. "But I know that something happened."

Major Gendreau sighed inwardly and got comfortable in his chair.

"Please explain what you mean," he said.

Mrs. Sophie Mirand had been sitting at her dining room table, with the month's bills spread all over it. Being a single mother of an eight-year-old boy was exhausting enough, but having to work two part-time jobs just to afford rent made it even more difficult.

As she sat there, her son Albert walked slowly into the room.

"Mom?" he said quietly. "I need to show you something."

His mother looked up from her difficult paperwork. How was she going to pay all these bills on time?

"I'll look at your drawings from school later," she said. "Mommy's busy right now."

Albert shook his head quickly. "No, not my pictures," he explained. He then lifted up his shirt and showed his mother his chest. "This," he said pleadingly.

His mother looked at her son, then looked back at her paperwork. Then her eyes went wide. She turned back to look at Albert.

"What happened to you?" she demanded.

"It wasn't my fault," her son tearfully began to explain. "It was the aliens!"

Albert told his mother the entire story as it happened.

A few nights earlier, he was sleeping soundly in his bed. He had been playing outside the day before, having a snowball fight with his friends, building a fort and tobogganing, and was exhausted at the end of the day. He had gone to sleep early, about eight o'clock, right after his bath. He was looking forward to having a snowball fight rematch the next day, and dreaming of how he would get his friends good.

Suddenly, something woke him up. He looked over at the clock hanging on the wall across the room. It said that it was half past one o'clock in the morning.

But something was wrong. He could sense it, rather than see it.

As he looked toward the window, a light seemed to move from far away until it was right outside. Then, something came into his bedroom right through the window, as if the glass weren't there at all.

"Yoda"

Albert blinked. The thing that came through the window was a strange creature with pointed ears and slanted eyes. When it dropped down and stood on the floor beside his bed, he saw it was about three feet tall and looked a little like Yoda from the *Star Wars* movies.

Albert tried to scream for his mother, but he found that he couldn't move a muscle. Suddenly, he was floating above his bed, light as a feather. The alien guided Albert toward the window, then Albert passed right through it, just as the alien had.

Once outside his home, Albert saw a weird object about the size of a jet plane hovering over the townhouse. He thought that maybe this creature was from a UFO and that it wanted Albert for some reason. The flying object was a grey craft, V-shaped like the tail of a dove, and not like a "flying saucer" at all.

With the odd creature behind him, Albert flew up to the craft and a door or window opened in it, allowing them to go inside. There, Albert was able to walk again on a hallway floor. He was guided into a room that had pink or orange-coloured walls that were soft and cushioned like pillows. The room had an odd smell, as if it had just been painted.

In this room were five other alien creatures. They all looked the same as the one that had taken him out of his bedroom. They each were wearing long robes and five-fingered gloves that looked like rubber. Around their short necks they each wore a necklace with star-shaped pendants. Albert then began to hear them talk to him, but he saw that their lips were not moving. They were using some kind of telepathy or "mental radio" that placed their thoughts right into his head, like in science fiction movies.

"You will not be harmed," said one of the aliens in a dull but calming voice. A fine thing to say, after abducting him from his house!

Then, despite what the alien told him, the creatures took hold of Albert and put him on a table. A plate was put on his chest while they examined him, touching his head and other parts of his body with metal rods. Then one of the aliens put its hand over Albert's eyes. Albert suddenly felt very tired, and then he blacked out completely.

The next thing he knew, Albert was being carried out of the room and had been bumped by something, jarring him awake. He had no idea how long he had been asleep, but he felt funny, as if he had been sitting in the same position too long and his arms and legs were tingling.

The aliens now floated him back outside, through the window of the townhouse and back into his bedroom, where they gently laid him on his bed. Then, with the aliens watching him, he felt tired once more and fell asleep again.

The next morning, he woke up as usual but had a vivid memory of the aliens and what they had done to him. He wasn't sure if it was real, because it still seemed like it could have been only a dream. He didn't tell his mother about it because he didn't think she would believe him.

But a few days later, Albert felt a funny itching on his chest. He went into the bathroom and looked in a mirror. He was shocked to see a strange, horseshoe-shaped red patch on his chest. That's when he realized his "dream" must have been real. He went downstairs to tell his mother. She'd have to believe him now.

And she did. In fact, she was very upset about Albert's story and the mark that had appeared on his chest. She was worried that something terrible had happened to him. What was the government going to do about it? Shouldn't they be protecting their own citizens from harm?

That's why she soon called Major Gendreau to report what had happened to her son.

"So you see, monsieur," she said, "my young son was taken from his room by an alien in a UFO and examined by creatures on board its spaceship."

Albert's mother spoke to Major Gendreau of the Canadian Armed Forces for a long time on the telephone. He suggested that she take photographs of the mark on Albert's chest so there could be proof of what had happened. But Mrs. Mirand did not own a camera, so she asked the officer for some help in understanding what her son had experienced. Gendreau told her to take her son to their family doctor for examination, then to a police station where investigators could get more details and take photographs of his mark themselves.

Major Gendreau could tell after the call ended that Mrs. Mirand was not satisfied with his suggestions. But what else could he do? Alien abduction, indeed! Such things simply do not happen!

And yet, Major Gendreau thought, *if this is just a case of a child's overactive imagination, why did his mother take the story seriously enough to report it to the air force?*

Source: National Research Council of Canada, Non-Meteoric Sightings File, File N95/28.

Questions a Ufologist Would Ask:

1. In the first story from Canada, a girl was thought to have been levitated into the air toward a UFO. In Venezuela, a boy was grabbed by an alien, and in Spain, a boy was slapped by a strange creature. In this story, a boy was taken aboard a space-craft and examined. Why do you think these young people

were singled out by aliens, and why were some treated better than others?

2. So far, these stories describe encounters with very unusual objects and creatures. However, none of these stories are actual proof that aliens are visiting Earth or that UFOs are alien spaceships. The stories could be made up or don't really reflect what actually happened. Yet, the stories are remarkable and the youths in the stories insisted they were telling the truth. In the end, you the reader must decide if the encounters with aliens and UFOs were real.

3. Do you believe that UFOs are alien spaceships? Why or why not?

4. Why do you think that aliens may be visiting Earth?

5. Why do many people see odd objects in the sky and think they must be alien spaceships?

6. This case comes from government files, so we know that something actually happened and was reported. Many official government files about UFO reports have been made available on the Internet. See if you can find some of these documents by searching American, Canadian, British, or French government websites.

THE BOY SCOUTS' SAUCER
(Florida, USA, 1952)

It was a hot August night in 1952, and four Boy Scouts from Troop 33 in West Palm Beach, Florida, were in a car driven by their scoutmaster, Sonny Desvergers. They were on their way home from a Scouting event and were talking about a stock car race that they were all going to be attending soon.

"It's been raining a lot," said David Rowan, who was eleven and interested in car races. "The track might have got flooded."

"Can we go look before you take us home?" asked Bobby Ruffing, the twelve-year-old pack leader. "If we take the back road along the coast we can check it out and then come home on the old Johnson road to get back to town."

"Well, it's already getting late, and I still have to go the long way around to drop you all off," said their scoutmaster.

"Aw, c'mon," Bobby insisted. It's not *too* late yet!"

Desvergers knew the boys enjoyed their Scouting trips and their parents wouldn't mind them being out a little bit later than usual. The boys were always excited about doing everything from going to demolition derbies to going on wilderness campouts in the Everglades. They were a good bunch of kids, and he was proud to be their scoutmaster.

He didn't need much convincing. "Okay, boys," he told them after a few more minutes of coaxing. "Let's do it."

They travelled out to the race track and found that it was in good shape, but there were some places where rain had made large puddles on the asphalt. They decided it was not enough to cancel the race and were happy that their plans wouldn't be ruined. They headed inland and dropped off one of the Scouts at his house, then drove farther south through an area filled with palmetto bushes and short pine trees.

As Desvergers drove the remaining boys home, he talked with them about some upcoming Scouting events while he viewed the passing scenery. After travelling only a few miles, he noticed a light off to his left, among the low trees.

"Did you see that light over there?" he asked, slowing down, but none of them had seen it. He started driving faster and another light flashed briefly as it, too, dropped down behind the trees.

"What was that?" asked their scoutmaster. "Did you see that one?"

Chuck Stevens, who was the youngest at ten years old, said, "Yes! It looked like a crescent moon, and it went down into the trees!"

"I saw it, too," said David. "It was really weird."

"Maybe it was a flying saucer!" Bobby laughed.

Their scoutmaster stopped the car and said, "I think that maybe an airplane just crashed. If it is an airplane, then there might be people who need our help. There also might be some burning fuel near the plane. I wonder if I should go and have a look."

He started to get out of the car, but Chuck pleaded, "Be careful! It might be dangerous!"

"How could it be dangerous?" snorted Bobby.

"Well, in the dark, he might fall over a log, meet a gator, or maybe the fuel fire could flare suddenly," answered Chuck.

"A gator!" cried David. "Oh, no!"

Desvergers didn't really want to leave the boys in the car, so he stood holding on to the door while he made up his mind. He realized that if there really was some danger, the last place that the boys should be was in the middle of it, despite their Scout training. He got back in the car and started driving again, but changed his mind and stopped once more.

"I think I *should* take a look, boys. If it really is a plane crash, people might need help," he explained. "But I'll assess the situation myself."

Mr. Desvergers turned the car radio on and found a popular late-night program was just starting. He knew it was just a fifteen-minute segment on the network, so he had the perfect idea.

"If I'm not back by the time that show is over, walk to that farmhouse we just passed," he instructed the boys, pointing back down the road, "and get help."

"By ourselves? In the dark?" asked Chuck.

"You'll be okay if you take your flashlights and stay to the road," Desvergers advised. "I'll be back soon. I promise!"

With that, he got out of the car, zipped up his jacket, and pulled on his peaked cap. He reached inside the car and found his machete so that he could chop through the bushes more easily as he made his way through to where the plane seemed to have gone down. Then he turned on his flashlight, shining a beam far into the darkness.

"You'll be able to watch me as I head into the bush," he told the boys as he walked away from the road.

Soon, the boys only knew where he was in the pitch-black night when they could see his flashlight playing about the trees.

Bobby climbed partway out of a car window and stretched up as far as he could. "I think I can see his head and neck just above the small shrubs," he said.

"It's very dark," David said, feeling very nervous about the darkness outside.

As Bobby watched, he could see the beam of Desvergers' flashlight moving in and out of the trees, and he thought he could hear him hacking at branches as he made his way through the dense thicket.

"I think he's getting closer to it, whatever it is," he told his fellow Scouts.

But then, Bobby saw the scoutmaster's flashlight beam point upward to shine on something in the air, and he was surprised to see that it was reflected back down as if it had hit a mirror, lighting the ground.

"What did he find?" Bobby exclaimed.

"It must have been the plane!" David responded. "It really did crash. There's something in there!"

After the scoutmaster had left the boys and was moving among the bushes, he noticed an odd smell. An odour like sharp cheese hit his nose as he wove through the short trees. It was slow going and he had to use his machete frequently to get through, but he was making good progress. He thought he could see something up ahead, but he wasn't able to make it out.

As he went farther into the thicket, he found the air getting very hot and sticky, like being in a steamy bathroom. Puzzled, he stopped and looked up to try and orient himself with the stars in the sky. As a Scout leader, he knew how to find directions by looking at the stars.

But he was surprised not to see any stars. That was very odd, because it was a clear night and they had seen constellations and even the moon while they were driving from the stock car track.

Desvergers suddenly felt as if someone were watching him, and the hairs on the back of his neck went all prickly. The heat had become more intense. He turned his head to the left and right, trying to find the source, and figured out that it seemed to be coming from directly overhead. He shone his flashlight up and was shocked to find that something was blocking out the sky above him.

The scoutmaster backed up a few steps until he had come out from under the strange object. He gasped in amazement. It was grey and shaped like a huge saucer, with a dome on top and vanes on its upper part, like a jet-engine turbine. This flying saucer was only about ten feet above him and about thirty feet in diameter. It was about three feet thick along its rim, where there were what appeared to be portholes or exhaust ports all the way around. The strange craft was completely silent, except for a faint hissing noise that sounded like air escaping from a tire that has a nail in it.

He thought, *This is exactly like what is pictured in magazine articles and stories about flying saucers and aliens from other planets!*

As he stood there watching, Desvergers felt paralyzed, and couldn't even move a muscle. He thought about striking out at it with his machete or banging it with his flashlight, but his arms wouldn't obey his brain.

He was even more surprised by what happened next. As he stood underneath the craft, a door opened somewhere on the bottom and a ball of red light, like fire, floated down toward him.

He tried to back up some more, but the ball came closer and got larger, turning into a wispy red cloud. When this gas cloud reached where he was standing, Desvergers put his arms over his head to try and protect himself from the strange vapour. But it was no good. He passed out as the gas reached him.

Back at the car, Bobby saw the red ball of fire, too. He thought it looked like a Roman candle at a fireworks display. He saw his scoutmaster fall back and a red mist appear to float over him as the flashlight went out.

"That thing got him!" Bobby yelled. "Let's go get help!"

The three boys panicked and opened their doors right away. Rather than head into the trees where Desvergers was having trouble, they wisely ran back down the road toward the farmhouse.

When they got there after their mad dash, they pounded on the door so loudly the farmer and his wife had some trouble understanding what they boys were yelling.

"A ball of fire got Mr. Desvergers," David screamed, gasping for breath after all that running. "Let us in!"

"Please help us! A plane or a flying saucer crashed in the brush," hollered Chuck at the top of his lungs.

Not sure of what to make of the boys' story, the farmer called the police right away, who in turn contacted the local sheriff. Officials arrived in a matter of minutes, sirens screaming and cherry lights flashing. Soon, the adults were all listening to the boys tell their amazing tale.

"I think we all have to go there and see what happened," the sheriff decided. "If it was a plane crash, we're going to need as much help as we can get."

The lawmen and the farm couple drove with the boys back to the spot where Desvergers had walked into the thicket. By this time, nearly an hour had passed since the boys had run to get help.

As they sat in the car talking about what had happened and planning who should go into the area, everyone was surprised to see none other than the scoutmaster staggering out from the scrub. He was dazed and excited, barely able to contain himself.

The police officer turned to his deputy and said, "I sure don't know what happened, but I've never seen anyone as scared as this man."

"I'll make a full report," the other replied. "Then we should send the report to the air force. They'll want to know about this."

"I was knocked out by a flying saucer," Desvergers explained finally. He described the falling light, the funny smell, the metal saucer hanging over him, and the red fireball, taking many pauses for breath because he was so dizzy. When he managed to finish telling them the entire story, the police officers decided that he should lead them all back into the bush to search for evidence of what had happened.

Soon, the entire group followed him back through the trees to find the spot where the saucer had been hovering. They found Desvergers' footprints, then his flashlight, on the ground in a flattened patch of grass, still shining. But there was no sign of the strange disc-shaped craft.

"But it was right there!" Desvergers insisted.

They went back to the car and started to head back to town, where they would drop the frightened boys at their homes. On their way, they discovered that Desvergers' face and arms were burned, and his cap was singed.

The police had doubts that the scoutmaster had actually encountered a flying saucer, especially one that directed a fireball at him and made him pass out. It sounded so unlikely that they thought he had made the entire story up.

And then Bobby spoke up: "But I saw it, too!"

Source: Edward Ruppelt, *The Report on Unidentified Flying Objects* (New York: Doubleday, 1956).

Questions a Ufologist Would Ask:

1. Flying saucers have been described to have many different shapes and be of different sizes. How does the object the scoutmaster found in the thicket compare with the one seen by Máximo in the Spanish pasture?

2. Because aliens would act and think differently from us, something that seems like an attack from an alien spaceship might actually have been a way to communicate. Is it possible that the aliens did not know that the scoutmaster was even there and the thing that looked like a ball of fire was for testing the air or soil?

3. Do you think that, in general, aliens visiting Earth would be hostile or friendly? Why?

THE GLOWING RING
(Delphos, USA, 1971)

It was November 2, 1971, and although winter was fast
approaching, the fields around Delphos, Kansas, were still free of
snow and the air was still warm in the evening.

Around 7:00 p.m. the sun had set, but dusk was still giving the
sky a deep, blue glow. In a pasture beside their farmhouse, sixteen-
year-old Ronald Johnson and his dog were tending sheep.

It wasn't a hard job. In fact, Ronnie preferred being outside in
the field with the animals to doing his other chores, like chopping
wood or hauling debris. The air was crisp and Ronnie had already
done his schoolwork, so he had lots of time to enjoy in the pasture
with his dog. He kept throwing a large stick across the meadow and
the dog kept going after it, time after time. But this last time that
he threw it, the dog didn't want to go. There was something wrong.

Just then, his mother poked her head out of the doorway of
the old wooden house and called him in for dinner.

"Ronnie!" Erma Johnson shouted from the back door of the
house. "You come on in, now. My pot roast is going to get cold!"

"I'll be right there, Ma," he replied. He was distracted by something odd that was going on, and didn't want to leave just yet.

His mother sighed and went back inside the house.

"That boy never comes when I call him," she complained to her husband, Durel.

"Now, Erma," he reassured her. "He'll come when he gets good and hungry. You know his mind is always wandering off."

"Well, my mind is set to start supper without him," she snorted. "That'll teach him!"

Durel gazed longingly at the steaming pot roast in the middle of the table. "Maybe you're right, Erma. I can't wait to dig into your cooking! Sure smells good!"

"Good," she snapped. "Sit yourself down and we can have a nice dinner, just the two of us. Ronnie can have whatever you don't gobble down!"

But Ronnie wasn't thinking about dinner. He was concentrating on figuring out where a strange rumbling sound was coming from. The sheep were trotting around nervously in circles in the field, spooked by whatever was making the noise, and his dog was whining, hiding against the fence.

Suddenly, a bright group of coloured lights appeared in a small grove of trees just beyond the sheep pen, not more than seventy-five feet away. Ronnie saw that the lights were on a weird, mushroom-shaped object about ten feet wide and just as tall. It looked as if it were floating or hovering about two feet above the ground.

The object was giving off bright blue, red, and orange light — so bright that it made everything seem like daytime, and he thought he could see every blade of grass on the ground underneath it. The light was so bright that Ronnie's eyes stung.

While it was there, the sheep were baa-ing and making quite a racket, very upset that this strange thing had invaded their pasture.

After a few minutes, the light shining from underneath the object tripled in brightness and the low rumbling Ronnie had been hearing all along changed pitch and became a high whine. The light became so intense that Ronnie was blinded and couldn't see anything else around him. He heard the sound of the object move to the side, heading south and passing right by his house as it barely cleared their tool shed.

His vision soon cleared and Ronnie could finally see the object far up in the sky, still shining bright colours. He decided to get his parents to look and see the thing, too. They would be so amazed!

Ronnie ran to the house and burst inside, where his parents were just finishing dinner.

"Ma, Pa!" he exclaimed. "This bright thing with colours all around just took off from the sheep pen and just missed the shed! It was sure loud!"

"It's about time you came in for supper," his mother said, ignoring his outburst. "Go wash your hands!"

"But Ma —," he began.

"Mind your mother," his father sternly told him.

"But it's real," Ronnie complained. "It was behind the shed and now it's up in the sky."

"Oh, Ronnie," his mother tsked. "You know better than to make up tall tales."

"I'm sorry, Ma, but it's not a tale!"

Durel Johnson wiped his mouth with a napkin and stood up from the table. "I'll take a look outside. If there's something to see, I'll be the judge of it."

He went out of the house and looked into the air. Sure enough, there was a bright thing hanging in the southern sky, about half the size of the moon.

"Well, I'll be," he said loudly.

"What is it, Durel?" his wife asked as she poked her head out of the doorway.

"Come look," he replied.

His wife and son joined him outside, and the three of them watched the object, now shining a bright blue like an arc welder, moving off into the distance until it was out of sight.

"See!" shouted Ronnie. "I told you!"

"Darnedest thing," said his mother.

Ronnie led them over to where the object had been hovering. There, even in the darkness behind the shed, they could see a glowing circle of light on the ground. Some trees and bushes nearby were glowing, too.

His parents reached down and touched the soil within the ring, thinking it had somehow been burned, but it wasn't warm at all. In fact, it felt very granular, like salt, and when they touched it, their hands became numb.

"My stars!" his mother said, amazed. She rubbed her hands on her legs to get some of the glowing dirt off, and her legs also became tingly where the dirt touched.

"I'm going to get my camera," said his father. "I think there's still some film in it, and I want to get some proof that this is really here."

When he came back with the camera, he took some pictures, then called the editor of the local newspaper. But because it was already after eight o'clock, the editor didn't want to come out to look.

"It's not going to rain anymore tonight," he said. "So whatever's on the ground will still be there in the morning."

With that, even though they were all still amazed by what they had seen and the glowing ring on the ground, they turned in for the night and tried to sleep.

The next day, Ronnie and his father went into town to talk with a reporter at the newspaper office. They convinced the reporter and two other people to drive out to their farm to have a look at the ring.

When they arrived back at the farm, the Johnsons took the reporter and her friends out to where the mushroom-shaped object had landed. The ring was very easy to see, although it wasn't glowing now, of course.

The reporter measured it and found it was eight feet across, and the middle and outside of the ring were still muddy from rain that had fallen a few days ago. The ring itself, however, was about a foot in width and was dry as a bone.

Not only that, but it looked as though when the strange object had landed, it crushed a dead tree and had broken a branch of a living tree, too. The broken branch looked very strange, because although it was still quite alive and had only been broken the night before, it snapped as if it had been dead for a long time, even though it was green under the bark and still had green leaves attached.

The reporter contacted the sheriff, who dispatched a state trooper and his undersheriff to see the ring for themselves. They took a sample of the ring and noted that the glowing powder on the dirt was white in colour. They used a radiation counter that they had in their trunk to check the sample and found it was safe. The glowing wasn't from radiation, at least!

The sheriff contacted the Center for UFO Studies, a group that investigated UFO sightings, based in Illinois. They were very interested in the Johnsons' story, but they were unable to send anyone to take a look at the ring for a long time.

Finally, in early December, almost a month after Ronnie saw the object, an investigator from the group drove out to Delphos and met the sheriff at his office, then went with him out to the Johnson farm. Because so much time had passed, the investigator didn't think it was likely that there would be anything to see anymore. But he was wrong.

He found that the ring was still clearly visible, even though it had snowed a few days before. He took more samples and did some tests. He discovered that once the snow had been shovelled off the ring, the soil underneath was still dry and crumbly, unlike the soil inside and outside the ring.

Then, as an experiment, he shovelled off part of the ring so that the white part was exposed, then poured water on it. Everyone was amazed when the water ran off the ring and refused to soak in.

Over the next few months, more samples were taken and more tests were performed on them. Some scientists found that the white material was very unusual and had no explanation for what could have caused the ring to form. Some suggested that the white stuff was a kind of fungus that grows on decaying soil, and that it would seem to glow when a light was shone on it.

Others were not so sure. People who doubted that the Johnsons had seen anything learned that the case was in the running for a fifty-thousand-dollar prize for "Best UFO Case" as picked by a newspaper. They suggested that the Johnsons were in need of some money to keep their farm going. Could they have simply made up the story together, as a family, just to try and make some money?

Ronnie Johnson says no.

"I saw the flying saucer!" he insists.

Source: Jerome Clark, *The UFO Book* (Toronto: Visible Ink, 1998), 168–172.

Questions a Ufologist Would Ask:

1. Marks on the ground thought to be caused by UFOs are called "physical traces." Some investigators of such markings think that they are caused by heat, radiation, or other effects from UFOs. Physical traces can be in the form of holes in the ground (from landing gear), burned grass or other vegetation, broken branches, or radioactive debris. Such markings were very common at reported UFO landing sites for many years until about 1980, when crop circles began being widely reported. Since then, physical traces reported at UFO sites have been very rare. Why do you think this might be?

2. What do you think caused the glowing ring? Was it made by a flying saucer or was it some kind of natural effect caused by bacteria or fungi in the soil?

3. Would you fake a UFO landing so you could make some money?

BURNED BY RADIATION?
(Texas, USA, 1980)

It was December 29, 1980 — shortly after Christmas. Houses were still decorated with lights, and people still had their Christmas trees up, draped with tinsel, some strung with popcorn. Presents had been unwrapped and toys had already been played with so much that their batteries were almost already drained. Things were starting to get back to normal — but not everything.

It was just after supper when Betty Cash and her friend Vickie Landrum decided they would go to a bingo hall to play a game or two. They often went out to do this in the evenings, because it got them out of the house and meant they weren't just sitting in front of the television. They made it their time for socializing, meeting their friends, talking about the week, and maybe even hearing some good gossip.

However, Betty and Vickie didn't realize that all the bingo halls in this part of Texas would be closed for the Christmas season. They went to their favourite one, but it was all dark and there were no cars in the parking lot.

"That's funny," said Betty. "This place is usually the busiest in the county. I wonder why it's closed."

"Maybe the owners are on a holiday up north," Vickie suggested. "I think I heard them say one time that they liked skiing. Maybe they went up to Canada or somewhere."

"I think I'll try the Longhorn — the one by the interstate," decided Betty. "It's not too far away."

But that place was closed, too. In fact, every one they stopped at was shut, so they decided to drive even further to see if one in the next county might be open.

In the car with them was Colby, Vickie's seven-year-old grandson. He enjoyed playing bingo with his grandmother and helped her place the chips on the right numbers as they were called.

As they drove in the darkness of the evening, however, Betty and Vickie eventually had to admit that they wouldn't find any bingo games that night. What's more, Colby was getting hungry; he was used to having his grandmother buy him snacks while playing bingo.

"Are we going to be getting some chips and Coke soon?" asked Colby. "My tummy sure is hungry!"

His grandmother laughed. "I swear, you must have a hollow leg! I keep feeding you but you keep as skinny as a cornstalk!"

"Maybe we should just stop at the next diner," said Betty. "I'm starting to feel a bit peckish, myself."

"Yay!" shouted Colby. "Soda pop!"

Betty pulled in at the next restaurant and they all had a quick bite to eat. While they were sitting inside and listening to the Christmas music playing on the restaurant's tinny speakers, they realized that they had been on a wild goose chase.

"Here we plumb forgot that it's Christmas and every place we want to go to is going to be closed on account of the season," said Vickie, shaking her head. She turned to Colby. "Finish up your snack. I think we're just going to be heading home."

Soon, they hit the road again, driving on a straight highway with tall pine trees on either side.

The sky was clear as a bell. This part of Texas had dense forests of pine and oak trees, with swamps and small lakes as well. It was very isolated, and not many people lived here.

Even though Texas never got too cold, the air had a definite nip to it this time of year. The car heater was on full blast, keeping them comfortable inside and keeping the windows from fogging up as they passed through a moist, humid area of swamp. Colby was starting to doze, snuggled up against his grandmother's arm.

As they travelled, the three of them noticed a bright light moving in the distance, but didn't think much of it. After a few minutes, however, they saw the light was coming closer to them, and was now taking on a distinct shape.

"What's that thing, Gramma?" Colby asked.

"I don't rightly know," answered Vickie. "I imagine it's just a helicopter from Huffman," meaning the air force base nearby.

"It sure doesn't look like a helicopter," said Betty, being careful to stay on the road while watching the glowing object slowly moving along just above the treetops. The road was narrow here, and the ground on either side of the pavement was soft because of the swamps. Betty realized that if she strayed off the road she might get stuck and they would be in trouble.

Suddenly, before their eyes, a large object appeared above the road just ahead. It was shaped like a giant diamond and didn't look like any plane or helicopter they had ever seen before. As if its appearance wasn't surprising enough, there was something even more amazing about it. It was shooting down bolts or streams of orange fire onto the road ahead, and they could hear a weird beeping sound that changed its tone when the fire came out.

"It's going to burn me!" screamed Colby. "Gramma!"

"This must be the end of the world!" his grandmother said loudly, with a trembling voice. She didn't believe in aliens or UFOs and thought this must be some kind of judgment from God. After all, here was a chariot of fire hanging in the air, certainly not of this Earth.

"Lord be praised!" she exclaimed.

Betty slammed on the brakes to keep from passing underneath the bizarre craft and into the fire. She managed to come to a stop, but the object loomed large in their windshield, hanging above them. It was so hot now in the car, being so close to the thing, that she had to turn off the heater and open the car door.

"Let's get out of here!" she shouted, leaping out. "Vickie, grab Colby and get him behind the car where it's safer!"

Colby and his grandmother left the car and crouched down behind it. The "diamond of fire," as his grandmother called it, was making a roaring sound as well as the beeps, and the heat coming from the craft was making their skin very warm.

Colby was frightened. He didn't know what was happening, and he wasn't feeling very good at all. His grandmother was crying, and this thing was scary, making a loud noise and blasting fire to the ground.

"I don't want to die! I don't want to die!" he shrieked hysterically.

"You're going to be all right," Vickie reassured him. "Let's get back in the car and we'll roll up the windows so it's not so noisy."

His grandmother took him back into the car and crouched with him in the back seat.

"Betty!" she yelled. "Get in here! Get away from that thing!"

But her friend wasn't moving. She was so frightened she was frozen by the sight of the unnatural craft. It was both terrifying and mesmerizing at the same time.

Then, as if things couldn't get more strange, they all began to hear another noise as well. The sound came from the distance, starting low then getting louder as things approached. *Whup-whup-whup!*

The three witnesses saw dozens of helicopters suddenly appear from all sides of the diamond-shaped craft. They flew in circles around it, like moths around a light bulb, and it looked as if they wanted to fence it in somehow.

The fiery object would have none of that, so it lifted high into the air and moved away over the trees to the southwest, with the helicopters chasing after it. The carload of scared people was left again in darkness and relative silence, as the roaring and beeping were gone and the whirlybirds flew away.

Everything seemed to go back to normal. Their ordeal was over — or was it?

Colby was huddled with his grandmother in the back seat, fevered and sobbing. Vickie was saying a prayer of salvation, glad that they were safe again.

Betty watched the lighted object and the helicopters disappear into the distance, then went to open the car door. It was so hot her hand got burned. When she carefully pulled the door open with a fold of clothing on her hand, she sat down inside. The car was still running, with the heater still going, so she switched on the air conditioning instead, setting it to high to cool them all down.

She drove ahead, wanting to get them all home as soon as possible. After only a few miles, they broke into a clearing past the tall trees and she turned onto the freeway. There, ahead of them, was the bright diamond-shaped craft again, shining orange like fire, and with many helicopters buzzing around it.

Colby had calmed down, but became upset that the object was again in sight. To calm him, his grandmother said, "Colby, help me count all those helicopters. How many do you see?"

"Um …" he began. "Two, four, seven, ten … There's so many!" The three of them in the car were able to count almost two dozen helicopters of varying sizes and kinds. Some had two rotors, some only one, but they all were flying together.

Finally, as the collection of helicopters and the diamond-shaped object move off, they lost sight of all the aerial activity and soon arrived back home, safe and sound.

But they weren't safe and sound. When she got home, Betty opened her door and went right away to the bathroom to freshen up. When she looked in the mirror, she saw that her face and neck were blistered, like from a bad sunburn. She was also feeling sick to her stomach, and her eyes were swollen as if she had been punched in the face.

During the next few days, she became so sick that she had to go to a hospital. The doctors didn't know what was wrong with her, so Betty had to stay there for two weeks while they ran some tests.

During that time she had other signs that something unusual had happened to her. Her hair had fallen out in patches, too. Doctors thought she might have radiation poisoning.

Colby and his grandmother were sick as well, but not as bad as Betty. Colby was sick to his stomach, and it was as if he had a bad virus of some kind. His eyes were red and watery for weeks, and some patches of his hair on the top of his head fell out.

Doctors decided that all three had been exposed to some kind of radiation, although they had no idea what could have caused it. Betty was diagnosed with cancer, something that had never been in her family. She thought it was because they had been too close to an experimental military vehicle that was leaking radioactivity.

Because they were so sick, Betty and her family hired a lawyer and sued the government for pain and suffering caused by their flying an experimental vehicle too close to them, but officials denied that they had any helicopters or secret craft in the area that night, so the case was lost.

There was simply no explanation for what Betty, Vicki, and young Colby had encountered that night. They were definitely sick following their experience, and they all saw the same thing, even Colby.

If it wasn't a secret military test, what was it?

Source: Jerome Clark, *The UFO Book* (Toronto: Visible Ink, 1998), 73–76.

Questions a Ufologist Would Ask:

1. What happened to Colby and the two women goes beyond the physical traces in the previous story. This time, there were physiological effects on their bodies. Some investigators of this case are convinced the UFO they got too close to was giving off dangerous radiation.

   This raises some interesting questions. Why would an alien spaceship be so radioactive? Most other physical traces or close encounter cases don't have high levels of radiation reported.

   Would aliens use nuclear reactors to fly between the stars? Most spacecraft built on Earth use chemical rockets to get into space and manoeuvre. Are there other methods that can be used to propel spacecraft through the solar system? See if you can find websites that describe alternative spacecraft propulsion systems that have been designed or built by NASA or other organizations.

2. If you were the lawyer hired by Vickie and Betty to sue the government, what kinds of things would you say in court? How would you argue that the government was not being careful about keeping Americans safe?

3. If you were the lawyer on the government's side, what would you reply?

CAN I HAVE SOME WATER?
(Conklin, USA, 1964)

It was the middle of July in 1964, and five friends were enjoying the summer afternoon by climbing and hanging around in the branches of a large apple tree. They were in a field on Woodside Avenue in Conklin, New York, not far from their homes.

The oldest was Floyd Moore, age ten. Then there were brothers Eddie and Randy Travis, who were nine and seven, and finally two more brothers, Billy and Gary Dunlap, ages seven and five. They liked this particular field because it had lots of huckleberry bushes, and the berries were delicious.

They were climbing in the branches of the apple tree, playing a kind of acrobatic "tag." First, one boy would climb up a high branch, then the others would follow him before he scampered to another branch. The first one to touch his leg was then "it" and the game started again, but anyone who fell was "out."

Their mothers would have been angry if they had seen the game going on. It was dangerous, and by early in the game, most of the boys had scraped knees and shins. Only one of them had fallen, but hadn't hurt himself too badly.

But boys will be boys, and Floyd and Eddie liked to climb as high as they could get, then sit in the branches and watch their younger friends struggle with getting up to them. Little Gary was the best climber of them all — his small body could squeeze through narrow gaps in the branches. And being lighter, could get much farther out on a branch than the others.

Floyd said, "You little squirt! That's not fair, shimmying out along that branch like that!"

"Is too!" Gary replied, sticking out his tongue.

"I can get you," said Eddie, easing his way slowly along the limb. He didn't want to admit it, but he was actually scared. He didn't want to fall and hurt himself like last year, when he fell off a tractor and broke his arm. Not only was that painful, but his dad wouldn't let him play with the guys for a month.

As they carefully tried to reach Gary, Billy was around the other side of the tree, on a different set of branches that was partly hidden from view of the other boys. He was ready in case Gary came his way and it would be his turn to be "it." As he was taunting his friends for being too scared to get too far out on the branch to get Gary, Billy saw a flash of light on the ground beside the nearby road.

Something shiny was among some tall weeds near the road that ran along the edge of the field. It looked like a big, upside-down bowl, and was about three feet above the grass. The rest of it was hidden by the thick weeds in the field.

"Hey, what's that shiny thing?" he shouted to his friends.

"Where?" asked Floyd.

"Over there," Billy replied, pointing down toward the road.

They all looked to see what it was, Randy and Floyd climbing down a bit and sticking their heads over some branches so that they could see it. Sure enough, there was a round object that was gleaming like a car's bumper, mostly hidden among grass that was at least as tall as they were.

"Whatcha think it is?" asked Gary, who quickly forgot that he was supposed to be staying away from his pursuers and had made his way down to them.

"I dunno," said Eddie. "It looks round and like it's made of metal."

As they all wondered about the strange object on the ground at the side of the road, they heard some weird noises.

Whee-whee-wheeyooo! came the sounds.

All the boys turned to look where the noise was coming from.

Whee-wheeyoooo! went the call again.

"That's a funny sound," said Randy. "It's like someone is playing a whistle."

"Or a kazoo!" added Floyd.

Whee-wheeyoooo!

Eddy pointed toward a tall tree about 150 feet away and not far from where the silvery thing was sitting in the field. "Look! That's what's making the sound."

When they looked over to where he was pointing, they all saw a small, humanlike creature about their size, only about three feet in height. It was high up in the twisted branches of the tree, far above the ground.

"It's like a little man!" shouted Gary, excited.

The odd "man" was dressed in shiny black pants and a black, short-sleeved shirt. Its face looked human, but it was wearing a black helmet on its head that had a glassy faceplate, and also two wires, like antennas, sticking up on top. There were two white, wavy lines across the chest of the creature.

"Who is that?" wondered Randy. "I've never seen him before. Is there a costume party today?"

"He doesn't look like anyone from around here," said Floyd, stating the obvious.

"I'll bet he's a spaceman." Gary laughed. "Just like in the stories about flying saucers I hear with Mom and Dad on the radio!"

"He does look like he's wearing a spacesuit," said Billy. "Maybe that's how he got into the tree. He flew up there from that silver spaceship down by the road."

"Well, I don't want no spaceman in our trees," decided Floyd. "Hey you!" he yelled at the little being. "Go away!" Floyd picked an apple and threw it at the creature, but it was too far away.

"I can hit him," boasted Randy. He grabbed an apple and threw it with all his might. He missed, too.

Soon, all five boys were yelling and taunting the creature, throwing apples, stones, and sticks toward it. But it was simply too far from them, and even though they were acting brave by throwing things at the creature, they were too scared to actually get down from the tree and get closer to it. The being kept on making the strange sounds, though, as if it weren't paying any attention to the five small Earth people.

"Hey! I'm talking to you!" shouted Randy. "Stay away from those apples! They belong to me."

"Those apples aren't yours," said Gary innocently. "They belong to the people who live next door to us."

"*Shhh!*" hissed Randy. "That spaceman doesn't need to know that!"

Suddenly, the little creature decided it had had enough of their antics and comments. It seemed to fall backward out of the tree and floated to the ground, moving in the direction of the shiny object on the ground near the field. The little being landed on top of the object and stood there, looking at them again. It started making its weird noises once more.

"What's he doing?" asked Gary.

"Maybe he wants something," suggested Eddy.

"Like what?" snorted Floyd.

"Well, it's hot today," thought Billy out loud. "I'm pretty thirsty. Maybe he is, too."

"Yeah, I'll bet he's hot in his spacesuit," added Randy.

Floyd waved at the little creature. "Hey! Do you want some water?"

In reply, the creature just stared at them and made its usual sounds. Then it floated slowly into the bushes, and the boys could see it crawling along the ground toward the silver thing.

"He must want something to drink," said Randy. "Let's go to my house and get some water for him."

"Okay," agreed Gary. "I'm tired of playing in this tree, anyway."

With that, the five boys climbed down from their tree hideout and headed to Eddy and Randy's house, which just happened to be in the direction away from the "spaceman."

When they got there, a bit out of breath because they had been running, Mrs. Travis was surprised they came home so soon, long before supper.

"What do you all want?" she asked, thinking they were going to complain about being hungry and demand a mid-afternoon snack.

"We need a jar of water to take to the spaceman," announced Gary helpfully.

"Yeah, he's really hot and wants a drink," said Eddy.

"A spaceman? Oh, what nonsense!" Mrs. Travis huffed. "Edmund Travis, you know I don't want you telling lies around this house."

"But it's true!" said Gary. "He has a helmet and a shiny suit and his spaceship is down in the grass."

"Did you really hear this spaceman ask for some water?" she demanded.

"Well, no," Billy said, a bit embarrassed. "He didn't actually say it."

"But that's what he wanted!" shouted little Gary, excitedly.

"Just wait 'til I tell your mother about your tall tales," she told Gary and Billy. "And as for you two," she added, talking to her sons, "just wait until your father gets home."

Yet Mrs. Travis was very puzzled. It wasn't like the boys to make up stories, especially one as ridiculous as a spaceman asking for water.

"Come with me," she said to Randy. "The rest of you stay here."

His mother took him into the bathroom down the hallway and shut the door. "Now, tell me what *really* happened," she directed.

Randy was afraid of being in trouble, so he told her everything about the little man and the silver thing. He even told her about Gary going too far out on a limb.

"I'm telling the truth, Ma!" he sobbed.

Then, she sent him back to the kitchen and told him she wanted to talk with his brother. Soon, Eddie was in the bathroom with her, telling the exact same story.

Their mother didn't know what to think. All the boys were telling the same tale.

She came into the kitchen and decided, "You're all going to come with me back to the field and show me where this happened."

"Yes, ma'am," Floyd replied, and he led them all out of the house toward the field.

When Mrs. Travis got there, there was no sign of the silver thing or the little man. But what she saw was very odd, anyway. There, where the boys told her the silver bowl had been, was a round area in the tall grass where it had all been pressed flat, as if something very heavy had been there.

In the middle of the flattened patch was some dry, yellow moss that looked like it had been heated in an oven and was very dry and crumbly. And just outside the round patch were three holes, as if something had rested on three legs over the grass.

"Well, I'll be," Mrs. Travis said, wondering what had made the marks.

"See? I told you," said Gary, with a wide smile. "There really was a spaceman here."

Source: W. Webb, "Conklin (New York) Incident." In: Story, R., ed. *Encyclopedia of UFOs* (Garden City, NY, 1980), 246–249.

Questions a Ufologist Would Ask:

1. The behaviour of the creature in this story is different from that of creatures in the other stories so far. It didn't attack the boys or frighten them, nor did it seem to want anything from them at all. It's possible it may not have noticed they were even there. But in this story, it's the boys who were attacking the alien, with apples and sticks.

   Suppose an alien came out of a UFO and said, "Take me to your leader!" Who would you take it to? Why?

2. Aliens on other planets would eat different things than we do. Their stomachs (if they have stomachs) might not be able to digest meat, vegetables, or breads grown on Earth. They might not even be able to drink water.

   Our bodies are based on carbon atoms, but some scientists think that life on other planets may be based on other elements, such as silicon. These species may be able to live at higher temperatures, and may not breathe as we do.

The study of life on other planets or in space is called xenobiology. Scientists often imagine what creatures on other planets might be like. What do you think a Martian would look like? Would it have two legs like us? Two arms? Two eyes? Why not one? Or five? What would it eat on Mars? Would it have a mouth to talk with like we do? Why not draw a picture of what you think a real Martian would look like.

VISITOR IN SWITZERLAND
(Nyon, Switzerland, 1977)

Early in the morning of October 11, 1977, the Voulet family was starting to get ready for the day. It was a bright, clear, and crisp morning in Nyon, Switzerland, and the rising sun had already lit the snow-covered Alps that were visible through the windows of their home.

They lived not far from a highway that ran past their house and beside a maize field. The maize was very tall, as it was getting near harvest time. A power line ran along the highway, which led to the main international airport in Geneva, only twenty-five kilometres away.

Jeanne Voulet got out of bed to make breakfast for her family at about 6:00 a.m. Her husband usually rose about fifteen minutes later, so she had plenty of time to put the coffee on and prepare his favourite breakfast of crepes and cheese. Around 6:20 a.m. she happened to look up from her cooking.

At first, she did not think anything unusual about an object she saw low on the horizon in the south. It appeared like a silver "trout without fins" that was just to the side of the rising sun, as if it were hovering above the nearby Rivière Savoy. The object seemed to be about twice the width of the sun, and was not moving.

"René," she said to her husband, "*Qu'est que c'est?* (What is this?)"

He was just coming out of the bedroom after getting dressed for work, and glanced in the direction of the object.

"*C'est une avion* (It's a plane)," he casually remarked. However, his wife insisted it was something other than a common aircraft. She got him to look again, but he still said it wasn't anything to be concerned about. Yet Jeanne thought that the object was moving too slowly for an aircraft, and it wasn't making any noise, either.

Their daughter, Nathalie, who was thirteen, came downstairs for breakfast. She always enjoyed her mother's cooking before she went to school. She looked out the window and saw the strange silver "fish" in the sky.

"*Maman,*" she exclaimed. "*Regardez-vous!* (Look at that!)"

Her father was still unimpressed. He did not think it was anything important, and pointed out to them that the object was in fact moving slowly toward the south, passing their house far away on the left side. There was an airport not far away, and he was certain that it had something to do with activity there.

All three of them watched it from time to time through the south window until it was time to leave. René Voulet left for work, still convinced the object was an airplane of some kind, while Nathalie went off to school at 7:10 a.m.

Jeanne Voulet was left to herself and watched the object while she sipped her morning coffee. Soon, she decided it was time to begin her housework and turned away, leaving the strange object to move away without being observed.

Around 9:00 a.m., Brigitte Manon, the Voulets' nineteen-year-old niece, came downstairs for breakfast, stretching and yawning as she made her way into the kitchen. She was on a holiday, visiting from Belgium, and was enjoying the privilege of sleeping in later than the rest of the household. As she came in the room,

Brigitte saw the odd capsule-shaped object through the window as well, and asked her aunt about it.

"*Est-ce que le soucoupe volante?* (Is that a flying saucer?)" she asked.

"*Mais oui!* (Of course!)" said her aunt.

Brigitte went back to her room and returned with a pair of binoculars she normally used while going for nature walks. Through the binoculars she could see the object clearly, but noted that it did not have any features at all: no wings, fins, windows, or markings of any kind. It was not leaving a trail of smoke, gave off no light, and was not making any sound. It was just a silver bullet hanging in the sky low to the horizon.

The object had progressed in its slow movement until it was now on the other side of the house from where it had first been seen. While Brigitte was watching it, the Voulets' neighbour, Mrs. Morrissette, came over and the three women watched it together. The older women then went into the other room to have a talk, bored somewhat with the strange craft.

As Brigitte watched by herself, the object suddenly split into three sections. Each one looked like a small, oval cloud with black spots at the ends. She called to her aunt and their neighbour, who both came back and looked with her out the window. They all saw the three objects where the single one had been, and then watched as the objects each took a different direction and moved away quickly, with what seemed to be a faster speed than airplanes.

As they watched, the objects stopped their movements and reversed direction, passing each other in what seemed to be playful "dogfights." The strange craft continued these odd manoeuvres throughout the day, and the women watched off and on as the afternoon passed. By about 2:00 p.m., Mrs. Morrissette left to go to the market in town, and only paused briefly to look over at the silver things in the sky.

"*Je ne comprends pas* (I don't understand)," she said to herself as she trotted away.

At about 2:30 p.m. Nathalie came home from school and she joined the others in looking at the objects moving in the sky. Suddenly, they saw some smoke appear to rise up from the maize field not far from the house. Through Brigitte's binoculars it looked like the source of the smoke was a small metallic "dome" resting among the tall plants.

"*Allons-y dans le champs* (Let's go to the field)," said Nathalie.

Initially, all three thought it was a good idea, but as they left the house and got closer to the field, Jeanne Voulet became frightened and ran back inside.

The two girls continued on until they reached the railroad tracks that separated their yard from the maize field. But then, even Nathalie was starting to get worried that, whatever the source of the smoke might be, it could be dangerous. Perhaps the air force had been conducting tests and something had gone wrong. As she thought more about it, she noticed the cats that normally stayed in the house had managed to escape and were now following them across the tracks. She explained to her cousin that she needed to turn back because she didn't want the cats to get lost.

Unafraid, Brigitte continued on by herself. She crossed the railroad tracks, went through the ditch, and walked along the edge of the maize field beside the highway. The smoke had stopped rising, but she was sure that she knew where in the field it had been coming from.

As she walked, she saw that a car had pulled to a stop near her and the driver had got out. Brigitte had been scanning the blue sky for any sign of the original three objects or of what had been making the smoke. The driver asked her what she was looking for.

She explained what had happened that morning and early afternoon and that she was on her way to where she had seen the object down on the ground in the maize.

The man said he also had seen an unusual object in the sky that morning. They talked for a few more minutes, then he excused himself and got back in his car. When he drove away, Brigitte continued on toward the maize field.

When she made it to the edge of the field, she was amazed to see something among the tall plants. Looking carefully, she saw that it was an odd person. As she crouched down to hide herself from view, she could see he was wearing a loose-fitting uniform, like coveralls, that was silver in colour. There were five buttons on the chest, and the uniform also had a hood, gloves, boots, and a shiny belt. Hanging from the belt was a baton of some kind, about six inches long.

From her vantage point about 150 feet away, Brigitte thought this person looked human, except for the fact that his skin was green.

She was so close that she could see his lips were moving, but she couldn't hear what he was saying. She realized with alarm that he had seen her and was likely speaking to her. Try as she might, she could not figure out what was being said.

Behind him, Brigitte could see a silver craft like a large car, partly hidden by the maize. It was shaped like a saucer and had a rotating light on the top like an ambulance, except that this light was green, like the man's skin.

Brigitte decided she'd had enough fright for the day. She stood up and ran away as fast as she could, heading for her aunt's house. When she was a safe distance, she looked back over her shoulder to see if she was being followed. Fortunately, she wasn't, but she saw that the silver ship had risen into the air. She could see now that it had three legs sticking out from underneath, but it had no other features, such as a door, windows, or other projections.

She was relieved to see that it wasn't giving chase but had flown away instead. She still continued running straight for home, seeking some safety in case whatever it was headed back toward her. When she got near the house, she heard the cows mooing loudly and the family dogs barking angrily, obviously upset by the object in the sky.

Brigitte burst in the door and excitedly told Nathalie and her aunt what she had seen, and they all discussed what had happened. What was that silver craft, and what did that green man want with the maize?

Jeanne Voulet telephoned the newspaper office in Nyon, which in turn contacted investigators. The next evening, a group of UFO researchers arrived at the Voulet house and interviewed everyone. They saw that Brigitte, Nathalie, and Mrs. Voulet were in a kind of shock following their observations of the previous day.

No one could explain what they had all seen in the air or what Brigitte had encountered in the maize field.

"*C'est remarkable!* (It was amazing!)" Nathalie told the investigators.

Source: http://www.ufologie.net/ce3/1977-10-11-switzerland-nyon.htm

Questions a Ufologist Would Ask:

1. The fact that the witnesses in this French case casually ate their breakfast while the UFO was visible is a bit strange. If there was a UFO outside your window, would you be so calm? Would you want to run and get your friends and

neighbours to watch it, too? Would you take photographs? Make a drawing?

2.	How could it be that so few people other than the Voulets noticed the UFO in the sky? Their farm was very close to an airport and a highway, yet only the one man Brigitte met seemed to have seen it and was puzzled by it. Why do you think the UFO wasn't noticed by others?

3.	How would you try to convince someone that the strange object you were watching in the sky was not an airplane?

THE BOY WHO VANISHED
(Voronezh, Russia, 1989)

During the past sixty years, unidentified flying objects have been reported from almost every country on Earth. While there have been many reports from North America and Europe, relatively few have come from places where information does not flow as freely, and so those reports have not made their way to Western media as frequently.

One of the largest countries in the world during the last century was the Soviet Union. News and information were tightly regulated, and the West was in the dark about much that was happening in that part of the world until recently, when the Soviet Union broke into separate democratic states.

With easier access to the country, people who study UFO reports found there had been many sightings of UFOs, some of them very spectacular and mysterious. One case in particular involved several children and teenagers who had close encounters with what seemed to have been aliens.

On September 27, 1989, something very strange happened in the city of Voronezh, Russia, about three hundred miles southeast

of Moscow. Dmitri and Vladimir, two sixteen-year-old boys, were playing soccer with their schoolmates in Yuzhni Park late on a sunny afternoon at about 6:30 p.m. It was a defensive battle, and it was a good thing that there were no referees to call fouls, or else there would have been many red cards handed out that evening. Shins had been kicked, and some boys had roughly pushed others to keep them from making their plays.

Despite this, Dmitri had just scored on the other team, breaking the tie.

"Good one!" shouted Vladimir, jumping high in the air. "We will win this one today for sure!"

As Dmitri ran over to him to celebrate, he looked into the sky.

"Hey! Why is everything changing colour?" he asked out loud to anyone in earshot.

Vladimir looked around. Sure enough, the trees, grass, and cement paths through the park were all taking on a pinkish tint.

"I wonder what's happening," he said to no one in particular.

All the other boys had stopped playing now, too, and were looking around at the strange appearance of things in the park.

As they were looking around, bewildered, one of the other boys with them suddenly pointed up into the sky.

"Look at that!" he shouted. "It's a fire in the sky!"

Dmitri and Vladimir looked up toward where he was pointing and saw a large red ball floating in the air. It was at least the size of a car, and it was moving back and forth over their heads as they stood underneath it on the soccer field.

They all wondered what it could be. It didn't look like any airplane they had ever seen, or a helicopter. It certainly wasn't a cloud, and it was far too large for a toy balloon, and too small for a hot-air balloon like they had seen at air shows.

Before their eyes, it suddenly vanished.

"Where did it go?" Vladimir asked, surprised. "Was that a trick of some kind?"

All the boys looked around the sky, baffled.

"It's over there now!" one of them finally yelled after several minutes. The reddish sphere was much lower to the ground on the other side of the field from where they had seen it originally. As it landed, the ball flattened out to a more disc-like shape. When it neared the ground, a window or hatch seemed to open in its side, which until now was smooth, without any markings or features.

Through the hatch came a frightening creature. It was tall — at least twice the height of a man — and it was wearing a silver, one-piece uniform with shiny, copper-coloured boots. But what scared the boys most was that the creature had three eyes.

Vladimir screamed in fear. "It's a space alien! Run for your life!"

The creature looked in the direction of Vladimir. Its eyes became very bright, like flashlight beams, and when it looked at the boy, Vladimir became paralyzed, unable to move or speak.

Everyone else saw this and became afraid. They began to panic and ran for cover, shrieking. Even some adults, who had been in the park watching the soccer game, became terrified and started running away. It was a scene of panic and chaos.

Somehow, during all the confusion as people were running for cover and trying to hide, the creature and the disc-shaped craft vanished. When they finally noticed they were safe a few minutes later, the boys and the adults slowly crept back onto the field. Vladimir, who had been left behind, unable to move, seemed to have returned to normal again.

But the worst was not over. As if by magic, the alien and its saucer-shaped spacecraft appeared once again, close by the group that had walked out onto the field. Not only that, but the creature was in the company of several other aliens who stood beside the football-shaped craft as if they were guarding it.

This time, the robot-like creature moved toward Dmitri and pointed a long tube-like device at him. It must have been a ray gun, because before everyone's eyes, Dmitri disappeared into thin air.

The alien chose not to pursue the other boys or the adults, who by this time were in a panic. Instead, it turned and walked back to the spaceship, then climbed inside and the craft took off. When it was out of sight, Dmitri reappeared.

"Where did you go?" asked Vladimir, concerned for his friend.

Dmitri seemed confused. "I ... I ... don't know," he stammered. "The spaceman pointed that thing at me, and all I remember is everything going black."

He looked around at his friends. "Where did the spaceship go?"

They explained how the alien had gone back into its ship and how Dmitri had come back after it had gone away.

"We should tell the police about what happened," stated one of the boys.

"No one will believe us," said another.

But later that night, when some of the boys told their parents what had happened, people *did* believe them. That's because many other people in the Voronezh area had reported seeing UFOs during the past several days. Reporters for local newspapers had spoken to others who had reported seeing a strange red object in the sky. When the reporters heard about Dmitri and Vladimir's experiences, they were interested and went to speak with them.

When news of the encounter with the robot-like creature got around, an official from the Voronezh Geophysical Laboratory, Genrikh Silanov, investigated the story. He went to Yuzhni Park on October 3, less than a week later, and looked for evidence.

107

Silanov examined the ground, the trees, the paved sidewalks, and anywhere else that he thought might have traces to show something had happened. He used a video camera to record interviews with the boys, who told him what they had seen and felt while the alien and UFO had been in the park with them.

He was amazed at what he heard. Dmitri and Vladimir were not the only witnesses to what the other boys and adults had seen on September 27. Silanov found dozens of children who had seen things in and around the park for many days before and after.

Some of the UFOs they had seen were round. Others were triangles. Still others were flat like pancakes standing on stilt-like legs on the grass.

Some teenagers said they had seen strange creatures with black, evil-looking eyes that moved through trees and other solid objects as if they were ghosts. Instead of the giant robot that terrorized Dmitri and his friends, some children saw a small dwarflike creature with grey skin, wearing a loose-fitting blue raincoat.

As newspapers and television news reports carried more and more stories in the media, more people came forward with stories of encounters with aliens and UFOs. People were getting scared to be in the park. Government investigators had no choice but to visit the park and meet with witnesses, take samples of "landing marks," and monitor activity in the area. Police were called in to help with investigations.

The Soviet national news agency, TASS, took the reports seriously and ran many news stories about the Voronezh aliens and the UFOs that had been seen there. There were TV specials and front-page headlines in newspapers about the events there.

It was several weeks before Dmitri and Vladimir went back to the park to play soccer again.

"Do you think we'll see that robot again?" Dmitri asked his friend.

"I hope not. But if we do, I'll be ready for it." Vladimir showed him a baseball bat he had brought from home. "I'll hit him with this before he gets me with his laser beam!"

Source: Paul Stonehill, *The Soviet UFO Files* (Surrey, UK: CLB International Publishing, 1998).

Questions a Ufologist Would Ask:

1. Many elements of this story seem fantastic and straight out of a science fiction movie. Ray guns, people vanishing, and giant robots make some people doubt this story completely. Do you believe this story about the boy vanishing when he was hit with a ray from the robot? Why or why not?

2. How would you explain this case, if you were a UFO investigator?

3. Do you think that sometimes, newspaper and TV reporters will make up stories?

4. Do you think that some people make up stories so that they can get into the newspaper or on TV?

THE SCHOOLYARD SAUCER
(Ruwa, Zimbabwe, 1994)

It was **Friday morning, September 16, 1994,** at about 10:15 a.m. Teachers at the Ariel School in Ruwa (not far from Harare) in Zimbabwe were having a morning meeting while their sixty-two students between the ages of five and twelve years old played in the schoolyard during their regular mid-morning break. There was nothing special about the day or their meeting, and some teachers were already discussing what they were going to be doing on the weekend, looking forward to a break even though it was so early in the school year.

Among the children massed in the schoolyard was ten-year-old Chris, who was playing soccer with his friends in a field next to the old wooden building.

"Pass it to me!" he called to Barry, who was trying to get away from some of the other players.

"Over here!" shouted another boy.

"No, me!" yelled another.

It was a mad scramble as a great crush of bodies started to come toward Barry, all eager to get the ball.

As Barry hesitated before passing the ball to someone, a girl from the other team shot past between him and Chris. Her foot poked at the ball in just the right way to cause him to lose control of it, and she kicked it to one of her own teammates.

"Hey!" Barry cried. "No fair!"

The girl laughed and continued running, but then stopped and looked into the sky, puzzled.

"What are those things?" she asked. "Do you see them?"

"See what?" Chris said. He was concentrating on the game and was hanging back to cover another boy, who was hoping for a pass.

The girl, whose name was Rebecca, pointed up in the air over some trees. "Over there," she said.

Chris and Barry and many of the other kids paused their game to look into the sky and saw what she was talking about. Hanging in the air high above the trees were three silver balls. As they watched, the three mystery objects disappeared with a flash of light.

"Were those balloons?" wondered Chris out loud.

"No, they didn't seem like balloons," said another boy. "They didn't have any strings or ropes, and they flew against the wind."

They turned when another of their classmates called to them. "Look!" he shouted. "They're on the other side of the school!"

All the students had stopped playing soccer and other games by now. Everyone was looking at the three silver balls that were closer now, but still up a good distance in the air, perhaps as high as a kite could fly.

Barry said, "They have flashing red lights on their tops."

"Those are certainly not balloons," said Chris.

As they all watched intently, the three objects vanished once again with a bright flash of light.

"It's a miracle!" gasped a young girl.

"Maybe it's the Holy Mother Mary coming to visit us!" exclaimed one of the other girls, who was very religious.

Then, the three metallic balls appeared once again, this time not far above the school.

"What magic is this?" asked one boy.

"They must be *ruserwa* (flying saucers)," said another.

"Oh, no," said a girl. "These are not flat at all, but more like our soccer ball!"

One of the objects started getting lower to the ground, following a row of electrical power lines on towers. It eventually moved down into a field just beyond the schoolyard. This area was only partly cleared of vegetation, with many gum trees, thorn bushes, and tall grass with cut bamboo sticking up from the earth.

"It's landed in the bad place!" shouted Rebecca.

She was right. Even though there was no fence or wire between the schoolyard and that area, everyone knew it was out of bounds. It was full of poisonous snakes, spiders, and dangerous animals, and there was only a thin path that workmen used to get into that uneven ground to service the power lines. If you walked into there, even a little way, you would be quickly hidden from view by the trees and bushes, and no one would be able to see if you needed help. None of the children ever went near there.

The object that landed must have been raised up off the ground somehow, or perhaps it was just much larger than they had thought, because they could see its upper part above and between some bushes. It was only about one hundred yards away from the schoolyard boundary, so the students could see it fairly well.

As all sixty-two students watched, two small men or humanlike creatures appeared at the top of the object and climbed down. As the pair of odd beings scrambled across the difficult ground toward the schoolyard, the children were all able to get a better look at them.

The strange little men were dressed all in black and also had long, black hair that hung down their backs. Their faces were horrific; they had large black eyes that "bugged out" of their heads, very small noses, and small mouths that were barely slits in their pale, grey faces.

The younger students in the schoolyard were very frightened by now. One boy about five years old ran away from that part of the schoolyard, crying, "Help me! Help me!"

Chris stopped him as he came by. "Why are you so scared?" he asked the little one.

"They are coming to eat us!" said the youngster.

"What?" Chris said, shocked. "Why do you say that?"

"Because," the boy answered, "they must be *tokoloshies*!"

"What are *tokoloshies*?" asked Barry.

The boy breathlessly explained. "*Tokoloshies* are little demons that carry people away from villages to roast on fires and eat them. My papa told me stories about that happening in villages near here, long ago when he was a boy. He warned me never to go out at night because of them."

"That's just a story grownups tell to scare little babies." Barry laughed.

"My mother told me that *tokoloshies* are just little monkeys," one girl said, "and there is nothing to worry about from them."

"Oh, yeah?" Rebecca said angrily. "Then what are those things?"

"I-I don't know," stammered Barry. He had to admit that these two creatures were unlike anyone or anything he had seen before, and they certainly did not look like monkeys.

He and the others were shocked to see the creatures reach the schoolyard and walk right up to some children who were standing nearest the edge of the field. They were paralyzed with fear and didn't know what to do. Should they go and interrupt the teachers' meeting? Should they run and hide?

Chris couldn't stand it anymore. He made his decision and ran away from the crowd of other students and into the tuck shop just inside the door of the school. He knew that the headmaster and all the teachers were in a room deep inside the school, but that there was an adult in the snack shop preparing for lunch.

"Mrs. Robbins! Mrs. Robbins!" he shouted as he ran up to her. "Some little men are in the schoolyard with us!"

The school volunteer didn't even look up as Chris stood there, out of breath and very excited. "Tsh!" she said disapprovingly. "And what are they telling you? To go back out and play at recess, and leave your hardworking teachers alone, no doubt!"

"No, no!" he insisted. "The big-eyed men came down from the sky and now they are with us! Please, come outside and see!"

Mrs. Robbins turned to look at him, becoming angry. "Christopher Ibekwe," she ordered, "stop telling silly stories and get back outside! You know students are not allowed in school while the headmaster is meeting with teachers during recess."

Chris started to say something, but thought better of it. He knew she was not going to believe him. He plodded back outside obediently.

He learned from the other students that while he was inside talking with the school volunteer, the little men had trotted up to some children and were speaking with them. But not really "speaking." As Rebecca described it later, "It was like they were putting words in my head. Their mouths didn't move but I could still hear them telling me things."

After several minutes of visiting, it suddenly seemed like the little men had become bored with the children. They left the schoolyard and went back across the out-of-bounds area to where their odd craft remained. Soon, the children could see them get back into the silver egg-shaped thing through a hatch in the top, and it rose into the air. It flew away and was out of sight in a matter of seconds.

Right about this time, the mid-morning break was over and one of the teachers came out to announce that it was time for the students to go back inside. She found they wasted no time in running through the doorway — something very different from their usual behaviour.

Soon, she and the other teachers found themselves surrounded by all the children who had seen the strange silver craft and the odd little men. It was such a din and commotion, with all the students trying to talk at once about something they had seen in the schoolyard. The children explained to their teachers, and later their parents and investigators, all about the unusual craft and the two small creatures.

"We heard you all yelling and making a terrible racket," said the headmaster, "but you are always so noisy when you are in the schoolyard."

"What did the little man say to you?" one teacher asked them.

A young girl, ten years old, said, "He said we were harming life on Earth with our machines and weapons."

"Yes, and we are making pollution," said another student.

"He said the end of the world is coming," Rebecca said.

The headmaster was not convinced the children were telling the truth, yet how could all sixty-two students have made up such a ridiculous story?

He had the children all draw pictures of what they had seen. Every one of them drew almost exactly the same silver craft, and their drawings of the little creatures were very similar.

The teachers learned that about the same time as the students had seen the UFOs and the little men in the schoolyard, a young man had seen an odd creature in Harare. This person was not the kind of person to believe in superstition or UFOs, and definitely not *tokoloshie*. He lived in a house on the north of Harare. Next to his home was an empty plot of land that had running water in a small depression. He had been walking near the water when he came across a small creature with bulging eyes that appeared to be startled at being found. The creature gave chase to the man, who ran away in fright as fast as his legs could carry him.

Could this creature have been the same kind that frightened the students at the Ariel School? The man never went back to that spot again, afraid he might meet it. He now believes in *tokoloshies*!

"Very strange stories, indeed," the headmaster said quietly, shaking his head.

Source: Cynthia Hind, "UFOs in Africa," in Hilary Evans and Dennis Stacy, *UFOs 1947–1997* (London: John Brown Publishing, 1997).

Questions a Ufologist Would Ask:

1. In almost every culture around the world, there are traditions regarding mystical creatures who terrify people or cause trouble. In South Africa, they were called *tokoloshie*. In Ireland, some are called leprechauns. For some Aboriginal Canadians, the wendigo is said to be an evil creature that flies on the wind and preys on humans.

   What are some of the mystical creatures of your own cultural tradition? Check your local library or browse online to find stories of weird, frightening, or playful creatures about whom stories are told in your area. Are they goblins? Yowies? Werewolves? How many can you list?

2. Have you ever been too afraid to walk through a dark field, yard, or building because of what you imagined might be lurking in there?

THE VIRGINIA GIANT
(Virginia, USA, 1971)

In late May 1971, three boys — Bobby Calvert, Mike Smith, and Johnny Tisdaly — decided to go camping in a field just outside of Fredericksburg, Virginia. They were friends from school, and they liked spending weekends out in the "back forty," as they called their favourite part of the rolling farmland outside the town. They got their gear together after supper, finished their chores, and said goodbye to each of their parents.

"Don't get lost again," said Johnny's mother. Although the boys were all young teenagers, she still worried that they might lose track of where they were if they set out too far from home. Two years ago they had got so lost that the state troopers had to be called in to find them. *But*, she thought, *that* was *two years ago, and they are much older ...*

"Aw, Ma," Johnny replied. "I know these hills better'n anyone now. Besides, I'll have Lucky with me."

Lucky was the name of his best friend — a big, playful German shepherd who loved to romp in the fields and woods with Johnny.

His mother gave him a big hug and sent him out packed with extra portions of the chicken pot pie she had made that day.

"That'll stick to your ribs real good!" she told him, and he was on his way.

By the time Johnny and Lucky had met up with the other boys, it was already nightfall. They quickly pitched their tents and gathered some twigs and leaves for starting their campfire.

While they did this, Lucky spent some time chasing rabbits, like he always did when they were out there. The boys could hear him barking and running madly off in all directions as he found new and different smells to chase in the darkness.

"I found some good-sized chunks of a tree trunk for the fire," announced Bobby as they set up their campsite. He held up a piece of bark-covered wood that was as big as a porcupine. "This'll keep the fire going for a long time."

"That's a good thing," said Mike. "It's going to be really dark out here tonight."

He was right. It was overcast, and there would not be any stars or moon to give them any sense of their surroundings.

Bobby laughed. "What's the matter? Scared of the dark?"

"Not with Lucky to protect us!" Johnny chuckled as the big dog bounded up to them. "Right, boy?"

"*Woof!*" Lucky responded, right on cue.

After a few more minutes, when they felt ready to start their fire, Mike pulled out his papa's Zippo lighter. He took good care of it and had promised to bring it back in working condition after their campout.

Soon, the campfire was blazing. They went through their packs and started making supper. It didn't seem like much: cans of baked beans and the chicken pot pie Johnny's mama had made for them. But to boys on an adventure away from home, this was a real feast.

After they had finished eating, Bobby was taking a swig of water from his canteen when they all heard a car horn honking somewhere down the valley not far from them. By this time it was very dark, and there was no sign of any headlights to show where the horn noise was coming from. The clouds could be carrying the sound a long way, and the noise echoed eerily.

"I wonder who's honking," said Johnny.

"Maybe somebody's in trouble," said Mike. "Maybe their car broke down."

"Or there's an accident," stated Bobby. "They might need help."

Lucky suddenly started whining and pawing the ground.

"What is it, boy?" Johnny asked him.

Lucky answered by yelping, then he lowered his head to the ground and scratched at his ear.

"Maybe it's his turn to be scared this time," said Bobby.

"Let's go see about that car in trouble," Mike offered.

"You two go ahead," said Johnny. "I'll stay here and keep Lucky company. He's acting kinda weird."

Bobby stood up. "Okay, I've got my flashlight. We'll follow the trail toward the briar patch. I think that's where it was coming from."

"No way!" retorted Mike. "It was coming from the south end of the valley — toward the Henderson's farm."

Lucky yelped again.

"You're right, boy," Johnny reassured the big dog. He turned to his friends. "You guys just pick a direction and find it. We'll be all right here."

Bobby waved his flashlight. "I'm the one with the light, so we go my way." He walked off across the dark field.

"Geez," Mike said, running to catch up with him. "Slow down!"

Soon, the two boys were out of sight, although from time to time Johnny could see the flashlight beam moving across the tall grass, so he knew they were out there.

"It's all right, boy," Johnny told his dog. "It's probably nothing."

But as he spoke, Lucky crouched down and bared his teeth, growling. Then, he suddenly took off into the field away from Johnny.

"Wait! Come back!" he called after Lucky. The big dog ran at top speed, then stopped about a dozen yards away, his back arched. It looked like he was snarling at something in the field.

Johnny ran up to him. He looked around and squinted into the darkness but could not see anything that might be causing Lucky to be so upset.

Lucky slowly walked further into the field, and Johnny had no choice but to follow.

It was very quiet. Johnny listened, but didn't even hear any crickets or June bugs. It was very strange. They had walked about halfway across the field through the tall grass when Johnny got a funny feeling in the pit of his stomach.

He stopped and looked around carefully. It was as if he were being watched by someone.

Johnny crouched down with his dog. "Do you feel it too, boy?"

It was so dark, and so still. Johnny started to get the willies.

"Nah, it's only my imagination," he said out loud to give himself more courage. He even started whistling, hoping that would help, too.

Lucky wasn't so easily reassured. His ears were tucked back and he was looking out across the field intently. Something was definitely bothering him.

Suddenly, Johnny felt something was there, off to his left. He looked and saw a large, glowing object rising up out of the field beside a nearby pond. It was flat and round, at least twice as wide as a car is long, and shaped like one of his mama's biscuits. It was pale blue in colour, with bright white lights in a line along its edge.

Lucky was really barking now, running, stopping, leaping into the air and snapping his jaws.

As Johnny watched, the glowing thing started moving in their direction. It flew silently across the field, and Johnny saw it light up every blade of grass. As it neared them, several "legs" started coming down from underneath it and it sank down, finally landing in an open area not far away. Its legs kept it from resting on the ground, and Johnny could see the bottom of the thing, which was smooth and without any markings.

Lucky was still barking excitedly, but not wanting to get any closer. Johnny thought this was a good thing, since *he* didn't want to get any closer, either. But at the same time, this was exciting.

After the weird craft had landed, a door opened somehow on its underside and a figure came out. Johnny saw that it was like a man, but taller than any man he had ever seen. This giant creature had long arms and was very shiny, like a robot from a TV show. In one of its hands it had some sort of box that was lit up from the inside.

Once it was standing on the ground, the giant looked around. Then, it looked right at Johnny and started walking toward him.

Johnny was petrified. What was this thing going to do to him? He had seen enough TV shows and science fiction movies to imagine all sorts of horrible things.

But the giant hadn't counted on Lucky.

To protect his best friend, Lucky got brave enough to run up to the creature, barking and snapping at its boots.

"Lucky!" Johnny shouted. "Don't let it get you!"

The giant didn't seem afraid of the vicious dog at all. It stopped and held its ground, not moving toward Johnny but not backing up, either. It bent slightly at the waist to look down at Lucky, who wasn't going to let him get any closer and was protecting his master at all costs.

After a minute, the giant straightened up and stood there without moving at all for a few seconds. Then, with an odd, bouncing motion, rocking from side to side, it turned around and headed back to the craft. Lucky didn't follow him, but stayed with Johnny, snarling, making sure the giant knew not to return.

The giant reached the glowing object, then moved quickly up into it again. The door closed behind it and within a short time the craft had risen above the field and retracted its legs. With a slight whoosh of air, it flew quickly away.

Johnny sat there in the grass, shaking after his encounter. Lucky sensed his friend's condition, and huddled with him for warmth in the cool night air. Darkness came back to the field, and all was quiet again, until …

"Hey, Johnny!" shouted Bobby. "There you are!"

"We went looking for you when we came back to the campsite and you weren't there," added Mike.

As soon as the two friends reached Johnny, they could see something was wrong.

"Are you okay?" asked Mike. "You look like you've seen a ghost."

Weakly, Johnny said slowly, "Not a ghost, but a giant."

He told them what had happened.

"Was it a flying saucer?" Bobby asked.

"Drat!" said Mike. "We missed all the good stuff."

But Johnny didn't think it had been all that good. Except for his trusty dog's bravery — now *that* was something that was definitely good.

Still, he was shaken and the other boys thought he was as white as a ghost.

"Maybe we should take you home," said Bobby.

"Yeah," agreed Mike. "Besides, that thing might come back."

The boys decided they had had enough excitement for the night, and packed up and went home. They told their families about what had happened, but nobody seemed to want to believe them.

The story might have ended there, except that, two nights later, two of Johnny's older sisters were driving home along a road near their home when they started to hear a humming sound. It seemed to be coming from above their car, and then they noticed that some red lights were shining down on them.

They continued to drive, puzzled by the lights and sound, when the car's engine suddenly stopped running. Not only that, but the headlights dimmed and went out and the radio stopped playing. The girl who was driving kept trying to restart the car, but the battery wouldn't even let the engine turn over.

As they sat there in darkness, they were surprised to see a saucer-shaped object about fifty feet above the road. It was glowing a bright white and was motionless, as if it were watching them.

Finally, after five minutes of repeatedly trying to start the car, the engine finally kicked in and the car lurched forward. The girls drove home in a panic, because the flying saucer seemed to be following them.

When they arrived at their house, the rest of their family — including Johnny — heard the car roaring up the driveway and came out to see what was the matter. They saw the large flying saucer follow the car up to the house, then fly away out of sight.

For Johnny, it was the second time seeing the same UFO in one week.

Source: http://www.ufoevidence.org/cases/case806.htm

Questions a Ufologist Would Ask:

1. It sure sounded like Johnny was afraid of walking into the field in the dark, and letting his imagination run wild, just like in the questions section at the end of the last chapter. But in his case, something really was there! What was it?

2. Have you ever been camping, sitting around a bonfire late at night, when someone started telling spooky stories? That's probably what the boys in this story were intending to do when their own real, spooky story began happening to them. What are some campfire stories that you have heard? Are they tales like the "Monster Chicken Heart?" Have you heard of the Phantom Hitchhiker? What about "I'm Coming to Get You!" or "Old Man Gimli!"? Look these stories up, and maybe make up your own so you can tell them the next time you are camping with family or friends.

THE VARGINHA DEVIL
(Varginha, Brazil, 1996)

January 20, 1996, was a going to be a warm day in Varginha, Brazil. The sun was shining a bright golden yellow as it hung low in the sky, but already at nine o'clock in the morning the air was sticky and dew was everywhere.

At the main fire hall in the city, a shift of firefighters had just changed and the new men were sitting down for coffee when the station's telephone rang.

Sergeant Miguel Santos answered the line, expecting to hear a panicked voice describe a brush fire on the outskirts of the town. He and his crew had been handling many of those calls this season, and they hoped that it would not be too hot in the hills that day. But the call wasn't about a fire. Instead, Santos found himself talking with a very excited man about something different.

"Please send someone right away!" said the caller. "It's terrible!"

"Is there a fire?" asked Santos. "Is anyone hurt? Please, calm down."

"No, there is no fire," replied the man. "No one is hurt. But you must come quickly, and bring a net!"

"A net?" Santos said with amazement. Then he frowned. "Who are you, sir? What is your name, and why are you calling the fire department? We do not have time for nonsense!"

"Oh, no, officer. You don't understand," came the retort. "There is a strange creature hiding in the bushes next to my house. It is very awful!"

Santos sighed. He guessed what this was about. They had been called out to capture wild boars twice before, but not in that part of town, and not for many years. It was not especially difficult, but took up a lot of their valuable time.

"What is your name?" he asked again. "What is your address?"

The man, still excited, finally gave his name and told the fireman where he lived.

"Please come quickly," he insisted.

When Sergeant Santos and his crew arrived on their fire truck, they found a crowd of people standing outside a little area thick with tall shrubs and many trees.

"Can you get it out from there?" a young boy asked them. "It's a terrible thing!"

"The boar?" responded Santos.

"Oh, no," the boy said. "It is not a boar. It is a *chupacabra*."

The firemen laughed. Santos shook his head. "A *chupacabra*? You mean a 'goat sucker'?!"

"That is just a tall tale," said another fireman.

Santos and the other firemen rolled their eyes. For months they had heard rumours of a large, lizardlike creature with glowing red eyes and a body spine on its back. It was said to attack chickens, goats, and other small animals, sucking out their blood and quickly disappearing into the night. The first reports had been from Puerto Rico, but they soon spread throughout the Americas.

However, no one had ever caught a *chupacabra* or even taken its photograph. Scientists did not believe the reports of its attacks, and said that it was actually coyotes or wild dogs that killed the animals. But those who caught glimpses of the beast bounding away from a bloody carcass were certain that it was a real creature. Some people believed that the *chupacabra* was not only real, but was from out of this world, because it sometimes was reported near where UFOs had been seen as well.

As the firemen stood there, not sure of what to do, someone in the crowd stuck up for the boy. "No, officers, he is right. That is no boar, or goat, or anything else like that. It is a devil of some kind."

"A devil? Bah!" spat Santos. "I will show you that it is a boar, and not something to make up stories about!"

With that, Santos and his firemen entered the bushes, all wearing thick coats to keep the branches from scratching them.

The crowd heard them noisily tromping among the trees and calling to each other, then calling to the "wild animal" they thought was hidden in the bushes.

"Come here, you 'pig monster'!" Santos said to what he thought he had found.

Suddenly, there was a terrible noise, unlike anything the crowd had ever heard before. It was a cross between the squawk of a chicken and the braying of a donkey. A big commotion took place inside the shrubbery, and the firemen could be heard crying out in alarm. Finally, Santos emerged with his men, looking pale and very upset.

"*Madre Mio!* (Dear Mother of God!)" he managed to say. Then he shook his head to clear it.

"I must call the army," he announced, and he went to his truck and spoke for a while on the radio. He was calling for help.

Within an hour the neighbourhood was flooded with army trucks and soldiers. Some officers were barking orders to their troops, while others were meeting with the firemen to decide what to do.

"I tell you, lieutenant," Santos was saying. "That thing is not of this world. It attacked us when we went to grab it, and it is very strong."

"Leave that to us," the army officer scoffed. "The Brazilian army is trained for swift action."

Some troops were sent in only lightly armed because they didn't think there was any real threat inside the little park. They came out upset and shouting a few minutes later, demanding that more soldiers come in with them.

"But bring the nets we use to trap the wild cats of the jungle!" one directed.

The necessary equipment was obtained from a jeep and, before long, many soldiers cautiously went into the trees and bushes again, the lieutenant among them. Once again, there was much shouting and commotion. Then, a victory yell.

"We have it!" announced their officer, coming out into the open.

"What is it?" asked Sergeant Santos.

"Well ..." the lieutenant started to explain.

Many hours later, at about 3:30 p.m., three girls, each fifteen years old, were coming home from work. Liliane, Valquiria, and Katia had part-time jobs on weekends because they had to help support their families. They were good friends and had grown up together in the same neighbourhood.

"I can hardly wait to get home," Liliane said. "I am so tired!"

"Me, too," moaned Katia. "I need to get out of these clothes and into something clean."

Valquiria laughed. "You mean, you want to change into a pretty dress so you can visit your boyfriend!"

"That is not true," Katia objected. "I am too tired to bother with that silly boy tonight."

Their teasing continued as they crossed a wide open field not far from their homes. The field had patches of tall grass here and there, and as they walked around one of the tufts they were startled to see a strange figure crouching down on the ground.

"Eeek!" cried Liliane. "It's the devil!" She immediately knelt and began making the sign of the cross. Katia joined her.

Valquiria was not as frightened, but was frozen in disbelief at what she saw. There in front of them, only a few yards away, was a horrible creature only about four feet high, bent over. It was dark brown in colour, with no hair anywhere on its body. It had a large head on a long neck, and its face sent chills to the girls' bones. The creature had two large red eyes, with no pupils, burning like fire. It had only a small mouth, a tiny nose, but it did have three horns on its head.

"Maybe it *is* the devil!" screamed Valquiria. As she watched in horror, however, she saw that it seemed to be breathing heavily, and whimpering softly, like a baby.

"I think it's hurt," she gasped after a few moments.

Katia stood up suddenly. "I don't care! I don't want it to do anything to me!"

"Yes! Let's go!" cried Liliane.

"But perhaps it needs some help," Valquiria suggested, thinking she could see some pain in the creature's eyes.

"Then you stay and help it by yourself," Liliane told her. "I'm getting away from here as fast as I can." And with that, the Katia and Liliane ran off.

Valquiria realized that was probably a good thing to do, too, so she took off across the field. She headed straight for home, with the other girls just ahead of her.

When they got to Valquiria's house, which was the nearest, they burst through the door and met her mother, who was startled by the frantic trio. Breathlessly, they explained what they had seen.

Valquiria's mother was shocked, but decided she wanted to see for herself, so she insisted they show her where this creature had been. Reluctantly, they led her to where they had seen the devil-creature, but it was nowhere to be found. However, they all noticed a smell like rotting eggs that was lingering at the spot.

"It must have been the devil — it smelled of brimstone!" said Katia.

Later, when they had all returned home, they were able to calm down and try to understand what they had seen.

"Perhaps it was an old dog," suggested Valquiria's mother. "It could have been hit by a car and was getting ready to die."

"No, mother," her daughter stated. "I know it was something else."

As they got ready for bed a few nights later, they turned on the television to get the latest news. The announcer was talking about something that had happened at a hospital in the city.

"The army has admitted capturing a strange creature with the help of the fire department on Saturday, January 20," the newsman was saying. "It was taken to the Regional General Hospital because it was found to be injured."

Then a picture of Sergeant Santos appeared on the screen. He was saying, "It was a very horrible thing with large red eyes. We captured it in a residential neighbourhood among thick bushes."

Then there was an interview with a man who had seen it enter the bushes. "It was definitely something not of this Earth."

The newsman went on to say that a second creature was also captured near a field on the outskirts of Varginha and taken to

Humanitas Hospital. A day later, army men entered the hospital and took it away.

After that, no more information was given to the reporters.

"We cannot comment on what we captured," said the lieutenant. "It is a matter of national security, therefore we cannot tell you what we have done with these creatures."

"Oh, my!" said Valquiria. "We saw one of those creatures just before it was found by the firemen and the army!"

"The stories are true, perhaps," her mother said, quietly. "It could have been a *chupacabra*." She added, "But those are just make-believe, like monsters in fairy tales."

Valquiria agreed with her mother, but still, she wondered ...

Source: http://www.ufoevidence.org/cases/case498.htm

Questions a Ufologist Would Ask:

1. In this story we have another example of a mystical creature that frightens people and even kills animals. It's called the *chupacabra*, and sounds a lot like other mythical animals described in legends and stories of long ago. Are the monsters of fairy tales based on actual creatures? Could a creature like a *chupacabra* actually be a boar or a wild dog?

2. Aboriginal people of northern Canada tell of a creature called the *witigo*, which is said to be a large, hairy beast that tore hearts out of humans and lived in forests and Arctic lands. Could this have been a polar bear or a grizzly bear? Why or why not?

THE CRASHED FLYING SAUCER
(New Mexico, USA, 1945)

José **Padillo and his friend** Remigio Baca were riding their horses near Walnut Creek in a remote area of New Mexico.

José was nine while his friend was only seven years old, yet they were very comfortable in the saddle. Both had been riding horses from the time they were barely able to run, and, growing up on ranches, they were used to being out on the range.

On August 16, 1945, they had been sent out in the morning to look for a cow that had wandered away from the Padillo Ranch.

"It's getting very hot," said José, wiping his forehead. "I hope the cow isn't much further."

"*Si* (Yes)," responded Remigio. "We should find some water for the horses soon."

They had entered some uneven ground along an *arroyo* (a dry stream bed), and the horses were having difficulty — their hooves were not able to get a good foothold on the rough chunks of mud.

"Let's leave them here and go on without them," said Remigio. "I am sure the cow is not far from here."

"That's a good idea," José said. He tied up his horse on a cactus branch and his friend did the same with his own animal. "They can both graze here and rest for when we go back."

Off in the distance, José had seen a mesquite thicket, a good place for a cow to hide. They went in its direction, clambering over sharp rocks and cactus with large thorns. As they slowly made progress toward their destination, storm clouds had begun to form. By the time they neared the thicket, a loud *boom!* announced the arrival of the rain.

"Quick! Under that ledge!" shouted Remigio over the thunder, pointing to some shelter. "We will be safe from the lightning there!"

They waited out the cloudburst as it sent torrents of water down onto the *arroyo* and lightning bolts flashed around them. Such storms are common, but always short-lived. The boys talked for a while, watching the downpour turn the dry creek bed briefly into a fast-moving river. In a matter of minutes, however, the rain stopped and most of the water had sunk into the ground out of sight. Soon, the clouds lifted and the sun came out again.

They came out into the open and began travelling again toward the patch of mesquite. Suddenly, they were startled by more light, but it did not seem like lightning.

"What was that?" asked José.

"I don't know, but did you feel the ground shake just then?" replied Remigio.

"Yes. That must have been the *gringos* at the rocket range across the canyon," reasoned José.

"No, that was much too close," said Remigio.

They were nearing the mesquite bushes, and they were able to hear the sounds of a cow from inside. Sure enough, as they approached, they could see the cow — and a baby calf.

"So, that's why you wandered off, you silly animal!" Remigio laughed.

"Let's have our lunch here," suggested José. "We can eat while the cow cleans its calf."

While they ate, José happened to glance up, looking further along the *arroyo*. A wisp of smoke was rising from somewhere just over a rise in the desert scrub.

"Look!" he said. "The lightning must have started a fire!"

They put their lunches down and left the cow to tend to its baby while they went exploring in the direction of the smoke.

As they made it over a ridge, they stopped and gaped at a strange sight. There was a long groove dug into the ground, as long as a railroad train. And at its end, almost hidden by smoke, was a bowl-shaped object the colour of tarnished metal.

"*Ay carumba!*" said José with awe. "What happened?"

"Perhaps a rocket from the army base crashed here," offered Remigio. "Let's get closer."

They moved in to the crash scene, but found that the ground was very hot, as if there had been a great fire.

"I can feel the heat through my shoes," gasped José.

As they walked among the smoldering greasewood trees, they had difficulty breathing because the smell was bad and the air was unbelievably hot and humid.

Remigio noticed the ground was covered in patches of small pieces of shiny metal, but very thin, like the paper inside a cigarette package. He picked up one that was jammed between two rocks, and as he did, it unfolded by itself.

"Look, José," he called to his friend. "This tin is magic."

Remigio crumpled it together in his palm and let it go again. As before, the curious piece of metal opened up and flattened out without any help.

"What is this made from?" José asked. But of course, neither of them had an answer.

"Let's get a better look at that big metal thing," decided Remigio.

Easing their way over boulders and broken rock, they were eventually able to get within ten or fifteen feet of the object.

"I hope someone is still alive," worried José. He looked into a jagged hole in the side of the large, circular thing, and saw … Yes! There were some people inside, moving around! They were still alive! They were —

"*Santa Maria!*" he exclaimed, calling on Mother Mary to protect him.

Remigio shared his disbelief. "They are *hombrecitos* (little men)!"

There were several small creatures that had the general shape of people, but were not. They moved back and forth inside the strange object so fast it seemed to blur their features. They were barely bigger than the two boys, with no hair on their heads, and skinny arms and legs.

"Let's get out of here!" yelled Remigio. "I do not think this is a place we should be!" And he began to run away.

José was more curious and didn't share his friend's concern, but he decided to go with him so they would not be separated.

They both went back the way they came, leaving the gouge in the earth and its occupants behind. They passed right by the cow and her calf, and finally reached their horses. They quickly untied them, mounted, and galloped away.

When they made it back to their ranch, it was already dusk. They found José's father, Faustino Padillo, who asked them right away about the lost cow.

"We found it," José replied. "But we found something more important, too."

The boys explained what had happened and what they had seen. José's father was surprised at their story, but was more surprised at how they were acting.

"Calm down, boys," he told them. "You both are very excited. What you found was probably something the soldiers were using to test their rockets. They should be left to deal with it themselves. Perhaps we will go back and look in a few days."

Because it was so late, José's father tied up Remigio's horse and drove him back to his own home. But neither boy slept much that night. They kept thinking about the *hombrecitos* and the odd circular "rocket."

Faustino Padillo was true to his word. He knew José and his friend did not make up stories — they must have seen something. So, two days later, he called a friend who was a police officer and invited him out to their ranch to come along when he went with the boys to look into the discovery.

The four of them drove out in two trucks as close as they could get to the mesquite, then hiked in to where the boys had found the gouge in the earth and the strange craft with the little creatures. But when they got there, José and Remigio were shocked not to see any sign of a disturbance or a metallic craft.

"Was this where you said it was?" asked José's father.

"Yes," his son replied. "But someone has moved it."

"It really was here," insisted Remigio. "You have to believe us!"

"Well, it's certainly not here now," noted Eddie Apodaca, the policeman.

"Let's go farther down the canyon," Faustino said, showing much patience with his son.

As they trekked, they noticed that the ground was covered in shallow lines or grooves, as if someone had used a giant rake to even out the debris and rocks. And not too much farther, they came upon the metallic craft, although it was now resting at a different angle than when the boys saw it, and it was almost completely covered in dirt and branches.

"It's like someone wanted to cover everything up," said Faustino.

"Stay here, boys," Eddie Apodaca ordered. To José's father he said, "Let's look inside."

The two men climbed on top of the large saucer-shaped object and looked inside. There was no sign of any life at all. They came back out, puzzled by what they had seen.

"What should we do?" asked Faustino.

"I think you should do nothing," stated the policeman. "Your ranch is on federal land and you are paid by the National Wildlife Refuge. And Remigio's father works for the government, too. You might both lose your jobs if the army finds out you have been here."

They walked over to the boys. "This is probably just a large weather balloon that the army has been using for testing," Apodaca told them.

"But what about the *hombrecitos*?" asked Remegio.

"Maybe you did not get a good look," suggested José's father. "And if they were here, they are gone now. There is nothing we can do."

With that, they walked back to the trucks and drove home.

José and Remigio were a bit disappointed. They were sure that they had stumbled across something very important, but José's father was right. Maybe it was nothing at all.

They were even more surprised when, a few days later, some soldiers showed up at the ranch. They explained that a balloon did, in fact, come down in the *arroyo*, and to recover it and its payload the army needed to build a road over the desert scrub so that military vehicles could drive there safely.

"But don't tell anyone we are doing this," the soldiers directed. "It is a military secret."

José and Remigio watched the military transports and jeeps come and go over the next several weeks. They wondered what really had crashed into the desert.

"It sure didn't seem to be a balloon," José said to his friend.

"No," Remigio replied. "It must have been part of a rocket that went off course and crashed to the ground."

Many years later, when they were grown up men, José and Remigio remembered the events of that night.

"I am sure it was a flying saucer that crashed there," José told investigators. "Just like the one that crashed at Roswell two years later."

Almost everyone has heard the story of the flying saucer that was said to have crashed near Roswell, New Mexico, in 1947. Some witnesses insisted that they saw pieces of the craft being carted away by the U.S. Army, and that a "cover-up" of the event has been in place ever since. According to some versions of the tale, bodies of small creatures were found in the wreckage, and they are being kept at a top secret laboratory, perhaps in a place known as Area 51 in Nevada.

But José and Remigio may have seen an even earlier crash of a different spaceship.

"I don't know what we saw," José says today, "but I will never forget it."

Source: http://www.ufoevidence.org/cases/case852.htm

Questions a Ufologist Would Ask:

1. The claim that a flying saucer crashed in New Mexico in 1947 has been told many times and in many versions. In some stories, the dead bodies of small aliens were found in the wreckage and taken away by the U.S. army. In others, the aliens were alive and were taken to a secret base in Nevada known as Area 51. Some of the wilder stories describe how the aliens have formed a partnership with Earth governments and have given us things such as computer microchips and products like Velcro. Other stories detail how different alien races are competing for our attention and are at war for the Earth's resources.

   There have been several movies and even a TV show about Roswell. It's a very popular story, but without any physical proof to back it up. There are statements from people who say they saw or touched strange pieces of metal from a crashed object in the desert, but no trace can be seen today of anything ever having been there.

   If any of these stories are true, what reasons would there be for the government to cover up the discovery of a crashed flying saucer?

2. If you had in your possession a piece of a crashed flying saucer, what could you learn about its origin? What could this small piece of odd metal tell you about the creatures who made it?

THE SCARY CYLINDER
(Dandenong, Australia, 1954)

Sixteen-year-old **Janette Brown** was feeling the chill in the air that evening. It was early June — mid-winter of 1954 in Australia — and at 6:00 p.m., the sun was already down and the stars were starting to come out. A cool wind was whistling through the trees and Janette pulled her sweater tightly to her body, quickening her pace.

She was on her way to meet her friend Jeanette, who was three grades behind her at school and needed some help with her arithmetic homework. Their parents knew each other from a local club, so Janette's parents had suggested she help Jeanette with her geometry. The girls had promised to meet that night to do schoolwork, but they both intended to do more talking about boys than arithmetic.

Janette walked to the far side of their neighbourhood in residential Melbourne and stopped just outside the gate of a factory that was under construction. It was where she was supposed to meet Jeanette, and from there they were going to head somewhere quiet to talk.

She turned on her flashlight and shone it on her watch; it was about a quarter after six. *Jeanette should be along any time now*, she thought. *I wonder if she knows anything about the new boy in school? He's dreamy!*

As she mused about things, she heard a low thrumming noise, like a motorcycle engine.

She looked around to see where it was coming from. There wasn't any headlight coming toward her from either direction on the street, so she was puzzled by what might have been making the sound. Then she happened to look up in the sky over the factory.

There, hanging in the air over the end building of the factory, was a large, dark object. She could barely see it because it was so dark, but the streetlights gave off enough brightness that she could tell there was something there.

She turned her flashlight on again and pointed it up at the object. As soon as she did, it started approaching her. Suddenly, three lights on it turned on: two on each end and one on top. Janette could now see that the object or craft was cigar-shaped, but with some kind of dome or canopy on the top where the upper light was shining from. The thing was about thirty feet long and about half as wide.

Janette thought the lights that had turned on were pointed at her like rays or beams of some sort. She was so terrified that she felt as if she couldn't move.

The flying craft came closer and stopped when it was only about fifty or sixty feet away, practically sitting on top of the factory gate. Janette thought that it seemed to want to make sure she knew it was there. The idea that someone or something knew she was there made her tremble in fear.

The thing was so near, she could see that it wasn't just a large chunk of metal. It was made of separate parts that were in motion. Underneath, three large wheels were rotating and making clicking noises as they went around. They didn't seem to have any purpose like springs or gears inside a grandfather clock, but appeared to be just for show.

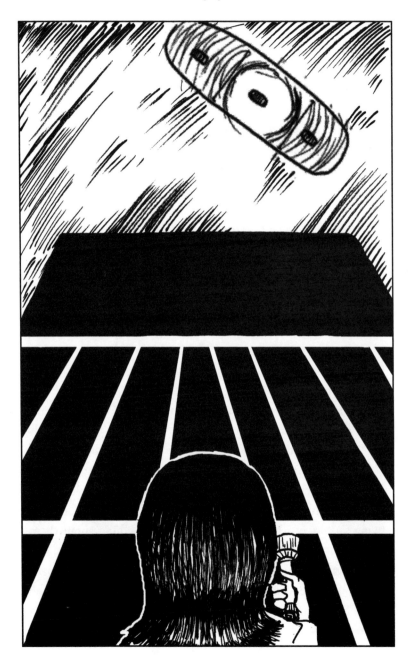

As she stood, transfixed, the headlights of an approaching car played over her. The airborne object must have seen the car, because it suddenly rotated and moved so that it could drop out of sight behind a nearby building. Could it be alive, somehow, and able to sense the oncoming car by itself? The thought made Janette shudder. What *was* this thing?

Janette was still shaking as the car passed and stillness returned. She was scared that the thing would rise up again, or attack her, or shine its beams at her again, or —

"Hi, Janey!" chirped Jeanette in her ear, suddenly.

Janette jumped a foot in the air. "You scared me!" She was so focused on the strange thing in the sky that she hadn't noticed her friend walking up to her, her soft-soled tennis shoes making no sound on the sidewalk.

"What's wrong, Janey?" Jeanette asked. "I didn't mean to frighten you. You look like you've seen a ghost."

"N-n-n-not a g-g-g-ghost," Janette replied, her teeth chattering and her nerves wound tight. She took a big breath and willed herself to be calmer. "A flying saucer!"

Jeanette's eyes went wide. "A flying saucer! Where? Where?" she spun around, looking into the sky.

"Well, not actually a saucer," Janette explained. "It's more like … like a tube or a cigar like your dad smokes."

"A flying cigar?" Jeanette questioned, dubiously, folding her arms in front of her. "I've never heard of that. The stories about flying saucers on the radio don't mention anything about them being cigars."

Janette was flustered. "No, really!" she insisted. "It had bright lights on each end and shone beams at me when it came over the gate!" She pointed over to where the object had dropped down when the car came by. "It went down right over there!"

Jeanette turned to look, and as she did, the large craft rose up again, with its lights brighter than when Janette had seen it. It was definitely a silver tube, just like her friend had said.

"Oh, my!" she exclaimed. "You were right!"

The strange object remained in the air, hovering in place, as if assessing the situation. Then, after a few minutes, it moved in a wide arc across the area and stopped above another set of buildings several hundred feet away.

"What is it?" Jeanette asked her friend. "Is it going to shoot lightning bolts at us or something? I saw a movie about that happening."

"I don't know what it is," Janette replied. "It's not a helicopter or a plane, and it doesn't seem like it's the Russians, either."

"The Russians?" Jeanette said with some doubt. "Why would the Russians fly their spacecraft over Australia?"

"Okay, then," responded Janette. "Maybe it's the Americans, and they're testing something new here."

"It sure is new!" said Jeanette. "I've never heard of anything like this."

As the two girls watched, the object started performing some odd manoeuvres. First, its lights flashed brilliantly, then went out so that only the light on the top and one on the left side were still on. The entire object seemed to spin around so that the remaining light was now on the right.

The object started moving, passing in front of them and across the street. It moved behind some trees and in a matter of seconds had disappeared from sight, leaving the two girls breathless and with their heads spinning.

"What should we do?" asked Jeanette. "Do you think it will come back?"

"I don't want to wait around to find out!" declared Janette. "Let's get out of here!"

And with that, they took off for home, with homework the last thing on their minds.

A week later, Valerie Johnston was still worried. Her daughter Jeanette was having nightmares about the strange, lighted object. Her friend Janette was also staying awake nights, afraid that "it" would come back and hover over their homes.

Valerie had contacted the Melbourne newspapers — not because she wanted publicity, but because she wanted to know if anyone else had seen the object. If it really had been flying over the city, she thought that more people would have reported it.

Unfortunately, the reporter from the *Sunday Telegraph* said there had not been any other reports that night. No flying saucers, and certainly no "flying cigars." The reporter spent an entire evening interviewing her and the two girls, getting as many details as possible for his story.

The girls stood up marvellously to the intense questioning.

"Our readers will want to know how you were feeling," noted the reporter. "What was it like to see a spaceship?"

"It was scary," said Janette. "I wished so hard that it would just go away, but it didn't."

The reporter was persistent, though. He turned to Mrs. Johnston. He asked, "Does your daughter have a habit of making up stories?"

That was the last straw for Jeanette's mother. "I can tell you one thing," she answered with an indignant glare. "I believe her story, even if you and the rest of Melbourne don't. Now get out of my house!" she added, shooing him out the front door.

When he was gone, Jeanette gave her mother a hug.

"Why doesn't anyone believe us?" she sobbed.

"They are just jealous that you saw it and they didn't," her mother reassured. "You know what you saw, and that's good enough for me."

Jeanette looked up at her mother again with teary eyes. "We won't be moving away where it's safer?"

Her mother pulled back and looked into her daughter's face. "I'll keep you safe right here!" she said with determination.

"Safe and sound," Jeanette agreed. She looked up to the ceiling of their home. "You hear that, spacemen? So don't come around anymore."

Source: "Teenage Girls See Saucer." *UFO Evidence.* http://www. ufoevidence.org/cases/case19.htm

Questions a Ufologist Would Ask:

1. How does the strange craft seen by the girls in this story compare with that described in others in this book? In particular, how is like the Scouts' saucer or the one seen by Brigitte in Switzerland? How is it different?

2. Is the object observed in this story similar to the one that may have crashed in New Mexico and was seen by Jose and Remigio? Can you imagine that the object in Australia in 1954 was carrying creatures like those seen by the boys in 1945?

3. Why do you think a government would be testing a new spacecraft over a city where people could see it?

ABDUCTED BY MONSTERS!
(Calgary, Canada, 1967)

David Seewaldt was over at his friend's house after school. He and Matt Grier had started doing some weightlifting every afternoon for about an hour. They were both fourteen, and they had started working out because they wanted to be like the wrestlers they watched on TV every Sunday night. Pro wrestling was very much "in" in 1967.

Matt's house was only a few blocks away from David's in a suburb of Calgary, Canada. His place was on the way home for David, and it was convenient to go over there before heading to his own home for supper. Besides, his parents didn't get home from work until about 5:30 p.m., so they had more than an hour to lift weights.

At around 5:45 p.m., David finished his routine and got his coat on.

"See you tomorrow," he said to his friend.

"Yeah," Matt replied. "Don't forget we have a math test tomorrow."

David groaned. "How could I forget?"

He left Matt's house and started walking down the block. It was November 19, 1967, and the weather was already changing to fall. There was a cool wind, and David shivered as he loped along, then turned and took a shortcut through a field.

Suddenly, he heard a humming sound, like a swarm of bees. He looked around and was shocked to see a huge, silver, disc-shaped craft with coloured flashing lights on its upper dome. The object was flying quickly through the sky over him, and he became frightened as it started to swoop down toward him.

And then …

At 6:30 p.m. David came through the front door of his house, pale and breathless. He ran upstairs to his bedroom, barely missing his older sister, Angela, as he zoomed by her on the stairs.

"What's the matter with you, stupid?" she shouted at him. "You're late!"

She followed him into his bedroom, and was surprised to see that he was crouching down beside his bed, nervously looking toward the window.

"What's wrong?" she demanded. "Did you drop a barbell on your head?"

But David didn't get her sarcasm at all. He was honestly worried about something.

"Is … is it gone?" he managed.

"Is what gone?" Angela asked.

"The flying saucer!" he replied. "It chased me across the field from Matt's house!"

"You're acting much weirder than you usually do," she said, shaking her head. "Why are you so late?"

"It followed me!" David answered. "It came toward me, and then … and then … I don't remember! I was coming in the door!"

Angela frowned. "Why did you stay at Matt's until 6:30?"

David looked at her, his eyes very wide. "But I left there at a quarter to six, like I usually do."

David told Angela about the strange craft with lights that swooped down over him, and how he became scared and ran home.

"But that would have only taken you two minutes," his sister pointed out.

A puzzled expression came over her brother's face.

"I don't remember," was all he said.

For the next week, David was acting out of sorts. He was nervous, looking over his shoulder all the time and getting startled when someone touched him or motioned in his direction. He sometimes seemed dizzy and disoriented.

His parents were worried. They had heard his story that night, too, after Angela had talked with him. She sensed that something bad had happened to David and insisted he tell them about it.

"What should we do?" asked his mother as they listened to the radio one evening.

Mr. Seewaldt was thoughtful. His son had not been his usual calm and easygoing self since that night. Throughout his childhood, David was not prone to making up stories and having a wild imagination. "I'm not sure," he said.

"Is there someone we should call?" Mrs. Seewaldt wondered.

"I'm not sure," her husband replied again.

Just then, a commercial came on the radio, announcing an upcoming program. It was about UFOs, and hosted by a man in Calgary who investigated people's sightings.

David's parents looked at one another.

"Do you think ..." Mrs. Seewaldt began to say.

The Seewaldts welcomed the UFO investigator to their home a few nights later. He was very polite and sympathetic, and talked with everyone, even Angela, about what happened the night David came home upset about being chased by a flying saucer.

The man talked with them for hours, getting as many details as possible and asking David questions to see if he could remember any more about what happened that night. Unfortunately, David simply could not recall any more details, or why he had been so shaken by the incident. The UFO investigator left, but asked that he be contacted immediately if anything further happened.

The Seewaldts went back to their normal routine the next day, and even David seemed to be calmer. Things went back to the way they were.

But in April of the next year, David had a bad nightmare. He was calling out in his sleep and moaning as if in pain. When his mother raced in to see what was the matter, she had to shake David roughly to wake him up.

When his eyes finally popped open, David looked at his mother with tears in his eyes. "Mom! Get Dad! I finally remember what happened to me! Monsters took me aboard the flying saucer!"

Mrs. Seewaldt was very worried now. David had never had nightmares before.

David's parents contacted the UFO investigator again, but when he heard how terrifying David's nightmare had been, and how he was now recalling seeing monsters, he decided to get some assistance. The UFO investigator sometimes worked with Dr. Kimball, a dentist who was trained in using hypnosis as a way of relaxing people before their surgery. He had found that relaxation through hypnosis was a good way to calm someone down who was upset or anxious. They reasoned that hypnotizing David could help him not be as scared when remembering details of his UFO experience.

Dr. Kimball had David and his parents meet him at the university office of another colleague — a psychologist — one night about a week later. After talking in general about what would happen, Dr. Kimball began the procedure of relaxing David for hypnosis.

"Close your eyes, David," Dr. Kimball directed. David did so.

"Now I'll begin by counting down backward from ten," the doctor stated. "At each step you will become more relaxed."

"Okay," David said.

"Ten," Dr. Kimball intoned. "Your eyes are beginning to feel very heavy, as if you can't open them any more."

"Nine," he continued. "Your arms are very heavy, like they were made of lead. Your legs feel like they are made of pure iron, and you couldn't move them if you tried."

"Eight. You are very tired; your mind is drifting off to sleep ..."

Dr. Kimball kept on going until he reached the end. When he reached "one," David was as relaxed as he could be, yet still able to hear Dr. Kimball's voice.

"David," he said. "Do you remember the night of November 19, last year?"

"Yes," said David, groggily.

"What did you do after school?" Dr. Kimball asked.

"I went to Matt's house to do some weightlifting."

"And then what?"

"I went home," answered David.

"What happened in the field on the way home?"

David didn't answer this time. He was trembling, and his legs began moving restlessly, despite the hypnotic suggestion that he not move.

The psychologist realized that whatever had happened to David in the field was too scary, so he tried a different tactic.

"David," the psychologist said. "Let's pretend you're watching TV. You're watching a TV show about what happened to a boy named David Seewaldt in the field that night. Since it's just a TV show, you can't be scared of what you see."

Dr. Kimball asked David again, "What was happening in the field?"

This time, David was calmer, and was able to describe what was going on.

"A big silver saucer was above me," he said. "It had coloured lights all around its middle."

He winced.

"What happened?"

"A beam of orange light came out of the bottom, right on me. Oh!"

Dr. Kimball continued his questioning. "What surprised you?"

"That beam pulled me right up into the ship!" David said, a little agitated but still fairly relaxed. "And there's monsters!"

"What do these monsters look like?" asked Dr. Kimball.

David's forehead became a frown, as if he were concentrating. "They're brown, and they're all covered with rough skin, like a crocodile."

"What are their faces like?"

David squirmed uncomfortably in his chair. "They're scary. They have eyes that go around the side of their heads, and they only have holes where their ears and nose should be. They just keep staring at me, not saying anything."

"What kind of clothes are they wearing?" asked Dr. Kimball.

"They're not wearing any clothes," said David, moving his head as if looking around, even though his eyes were closed.

"Are they big or little?"

David paused to think about what he was seeing in his mind. "They're about as tall as my dad," he said. Then David became more upset. "They're touching me! They're looking at my hair, my eyes, and my nose ... up close!"

David described in detail, with some difficulty, how the two aliens put him on a small, low bed, like a doctor's examining table. Then they held his head and looked at his body. During this time they made high-pitched buzzing sounds to each other, as if they were talking about David's body.

"Now they're moving me along a hallway into a room somewhere else in the ship," David said. "There's lights all over the ceiling, and they're putting me on a table in the middle of the room."

David twisted in his chair and said, "Ow!"

"What happened?" asked Dr. Kimball.

"One of them put a big grey thing on top of me and one of them stuck me with a needle. It hurts!" he cried.

The hypnosis session lasted for about an hour, with David reliving his awkward experience on board the craft with the monsters. It seemed that, after they had examined him, the strange creatures used the same "beam" to send him back down to the Earth. He then remembered running away as fast as he could until he reached home.

Dr. Kimball decided it was time to bring David out of the trance and wake him up. He calmed him down again, and counted upward from one, suggesting to David that he was waking up gradually until he reached ten.

When David was finally awake, he looked around at his parents and the two doctors.

"Did it really happen?" he asked them.

"I don't know," answered Dr. Kimball. "I really don't know."

Source: John Magor, *Our UFO Visitors* (Saanichton, BC: Hancock House, 1977), 165–170.

Questions a Ufologist Would Ask:

1. Hypnosis is sometimes used by psychologists and physicians to help relieve pain and calm people who are feeling anxious or upset about events in their lives. Hypnosis can help some people relax and fall into a deep sleep, at which time they can be suggestible to simple directions. We sometimes see hypnosis on stage as entertainment, and there are videos on YouTube of people who are hypnotized into thinking they are chickens or other animals.

    Hypnosis is an interesting tool, but it has its limitations. People cannot be made to do anything that they would not do while awake. There are also some limitations to what you can make some people remember and believe after being hypnotized.

    Would you ever agree to be hypnotized? What do you think it would be like?

2. Read up on hypnosis, and maybe go see a show by a stage hypnotist. See for yourself how a simple relaxation tool can be used to affect the human mind.

    If a person believes something to be true, would they still believe it if he or she was hypnotized? What if it really wasn't true? How could you tell if someone was lying?

THE MAN IN THE SILVER EGG
(Węgierska Górka, Poland, 1954)

Danuszka Lobchuk was visiting her cousins in Węgierska Górka in southern Poland. It was a bright summer day in 1954, and the perfect weather for four eleven-year-old girls to be enjoying a holiday.

At about 9:00 a.m., her cousins Jania, Olga, and Katażyna left their home and took Danuszka with them on a walk into the forest. They were given the chore of picking mushrooms for supper — a task they didn't mind because it gave them an excuse to explore the area and spend the day outside.

Danuszka lived in the city, and she did not have many chances to be in the country like this. She could see rolling hills not far away, with craggy rocks sticking out, and small brooks and streams winding their way across the lavender-covered fields. *This must be what it is like to be in paradise*, she thought. *It's so beautiful!*

"Oh, Nunu," Jania said, "do you see that hawk circling in the sky?" Nunu was the name that Danuszka's cousins called her for short.

"Yes," she replied. "Do you think there is a nest nearby?"

"It is probably in those rocks along the cliff," suggested Katażyna.

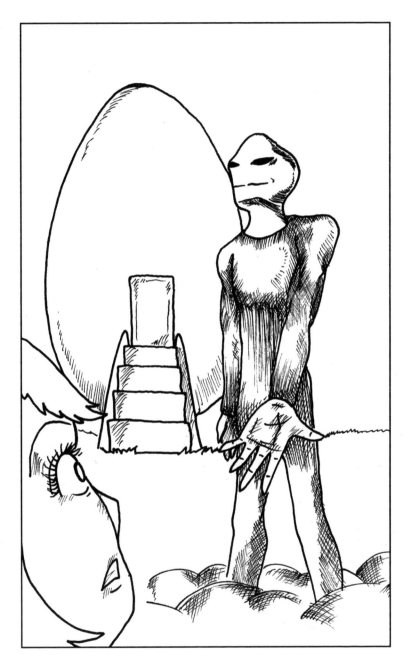

"Oh, let's go see!" Danuszka said.

"No, Nunu," said Olga. "It is too dangerous to climb there, with many loose stones, and there may be wolverines hiding in between."

"Look here," announced Jania. "I've found some nice mushrooms already!"

"Are those the good ones that *dziadek* (grandpa) likes?" asked Katażyna.

"Yes, let's hope we can pick enough that we can all get some and he doesn't eat them all!" Jania laughed.

The girls each found a nice patch of mushrooms and sat down with their baskets, tucking their legs underneath them, being careful not to soil their dresses on the soft ground or the dewy grass. While they picked the mushrooms, they gossiped and giggled and talked about their families and friends, and what they planned to do the rest of the summer. Mostly, however, they were talking about boys and teasing one another about which one of them liked which boy the most.

"I think that Nunu would like Piotr," said Olga. "He's perfect for her!"

Katażyna laughed. "Oh, Olga, you're so mean! Piotr has buck teeth and one eye that wanders! Besides, he works on the pig farm in the valley. He smells so bad all the time!"

But Danuszka wasn't really listening to the other girls. She kept looking toward the rocks near the cliff. She felt as if something was calling to her.

"Nunu!" Olga said, startling her. "See? She's already dreaming about Piotr!"

Danuszka laughed along with her cousins. She joined in with their conversation again, but still, she felt attracted to something near the rocks.

Finally, when the other girls had their backs to her, she seized the opportunity to slip away quietly and walk toward the tall rocks. There was a clutch of trees beside them, and in there, almost hidden by branches, Danuszka could see a whitish oval of light just above the ground. She felt drawn toward the light, as if it were beckoning.

She wove between the trees and bushes, and soon was in a bit of a clearing. There, she was surprised to see, standing beside the large egg-shaped light, a man — but not an ordinary man. He was tall — just slightly taller than her father, perhaps six feet in height. His face was unusual; his skin was normal in colour, but his mouth was just a thin slit with no lips. He didn't seem to have any nose at all, and his eyes were small and almond-shaped, somehow wrapping around the side of his head.

His clothing was very odd; it was almost transparent, somewhat shimmery, and parts of it were glowing a bright red. It was tight-fitting, and Danuszka could not see any buttons or zippers — not even any seams. She was good at sewing, helping mend clothes for her mother, but this man's clothes were perfect.

As Danuszka got closer, she could see that the strange man's lower body seemed as if it were surrounded by fog or smoke, so she couldn't see his legs clearly. Yet, he was standing next to the oval object, which she now saw was a solid object that was glowing like a firefly. He had one arm outstretched toward it, and Danuszka saw a small staircase in its side, leading upward to a rectangular door. She realized he was inviting her in.

Despite the strangeness of all of this, for some reason Danuszka wasn't feeling any fear or worry about what was happening. The man was very unusual, and it was very strange that this egg-shaped thing was sitting in the trees near her cousins' farm, but Danuszka was relaxed and calm, as if nothing was wrong or out of place.

She walked slowly up the steps and into the doorway — the entranceway was high, so she didn't need to duck her head. When she was inside she looked around. It was as if she were in a small, circular shed, but all made out of a shiny white metal, like pure silver.

Standing around the single room were four other men, similar in appearance to the one she'd met outside, although these men were smaller — not much taller than her, in fact. There was a pillar in the centre of the room, stretching from floor to ceiling. Light seemed to come from everywhere, and she could not see any light bulbs or lanterns anywhere.

"Welcome, Danuszka," said a voice.

She couldn't figure out who had spoken. One of the shorter men? Or the tall one who had now followed her inside?

"It is I," came the voice again. Danuszka realized the voice was coming from inside her head. The tall man was facing her. *He must be the one who is speaking to me … without words!*

"We are glad you have come to visit with us," said the man. He was speaking perfect Polish. It was a kind of singsong voice, but flat and without any rise in tone or emotion.

Danuszka had a thousand questions she wanted to ask. *Who are you? Where are you from? Why are you here?*

"All in good time," said the man, reading her thoughts. "Please sit down."

Danuszka looked around. There were no chairs or furniture of any kind. "On the floor?" she asked.

"Yes."

She sat and leaned back against the wall. But as soon as she did, she began to feel sleepy. It was all she could do to keep her eyes open.

Danuszka tried to ask what was happening, but before she could, she was fast asleep.

"Nunu!" Jania was saying. "Wake up! Where have you been?"

Danuszka blinked her eyes. She was a bit confused. Where was the strange man, and the big glowing egg?

Katażyna was shaking her shoulders. "Danuszka, are you all right? We have been so worried about you!"

She looked around. She was sitting on the ground in the clearing, not far from the rocks along the cliff. But where was the oval light? It should have been right there, in view of everybody.

"I … I was right *here*," Danuszka said, slowly. "And then I was in the trees with the shining egg. But there was a tall man in a silver suit here, too."

"We didn't see any light," said Olga. "Our biggest problem was that we didn't see any sign of you! Where have you been? It's almost suppertime!"

"What?" Danuszka said, startled. She looked at the sky. Sure enough, the sun had made its way across the valley and was now in the west instead of the east.

"Yes, it's almost four o'clock!" said Katażyna. "My parents will be wondering where we are. We were supposed to be picking mushrooms for dinner, and the rest of us have full baskets. But look at yours!"

Danuszka looked beside her. There was her basket. Completely empty, without even the few mushrooms she had picked before she went in search of what had been drawing her to the rocks.

"We have been looking all over for you," Jania scolded. "We've been here at this spot several times, and you weren't here before. Where have you been hiding?"

Danuszka had a feeling as if she had just been running away from someone, after a fight or argument. Her memory of the past few hours was very hazy. But she could remember being inside the strange room with the tall man and his companions. What had happened while she was asleep?

She quickly realized her cousins would not believe her story, so she decided not to say anything to them about it. "I was just further into the glade," she told them. "I'm sorry, I lost track of time."

"Well, at least some of us will be bringing something home for supper," snorted Olga.

When the girls arrived back at the house, Danuszka's aunt and mother were angry with her for not having any mushrooms in her basket, but things were soon forgotten as she helped the others prepare for supper. They had a lovely meal, with dandelion greens, *kapusta* (cabbage), *pirogi* (potato dumplings), and *wierprzowina* (pork) in mushroom gravy.

Later, before going to bed, Danuszka went up to her mother and talked with her quietly.

"*Matka* (Mother)," she said. "I must tell you about today."

"Why? What is it, child?" he mother asked. "If it is about why you didn't bring any mushrooms home for supper, do not worry. I know how a young mind like yours can wander when you're doing a chore. Your aunt and I were not really very angry."

Danuszka looked into her mother's smiling and loving eyes.

"But it was not like that," said Danuszka. "I met an odd man, and he led me into a bright, shining egg that was hovering in the forest."

"A man ..." her mother began to say, concerned.

"Yes," Danuszka answered, "but a very unusual man, with no ears or nose, and he spoke to me through my head without moving his mouth. And the walls were shining bright, and there was a pillar in the centre of the big room, and …"

Her mother relaxed. "Oh, Nunu," she said affectionately. "It is all right; you fell asleep in the glade and had a dream." She hugged her daughter tightly.

"But it did not seem like a dream," Danuszka insisted. "It seemed so real!"

"Hush, little *dziewczyna* (girl)," her mother said. "Forget about this. It is not important. And don't even bother telling your cousins about it. They will only tease you more!"

"But …" Danuszka started to say, then thought better of it. "All right, mother," she finally said. She wondered whether it all really was a dream.

In 1986, nearly thirty-two years later, Danuszka was watching television with her husband Piotr. She had grown up and married him after all. He had become a handsome man and had inherited the pig farm from his family — and was even rich enough to buy up several other farms as well — and they were now living comfortably just outside of Warsaw.

They had three children of their own, and the two boys enjoyed watching American TV shows like *Star Trek* and *The Twilight Zone*. Right after one of the shows, a newscast came on, describing the sighting of UFOs and aliens in Belgium, not far away. The news story had an interview with some children who had seen a strange, saucer-shaped object land, and later a small, grey-skinned alien figure beside it.

"Do you believe in UFOs and aliens, *Ojciec* (Father)?" one of their sons asked.

"No, of course not!" was his reply. "There are no such things!"

But Danuszka was suddenly reminded of her experience more than three decades earlier.

"I believe in aliens and UFOs from other planets," she announced to her family.

They all looked at her, surprised.

"Why, *Matka*?" her other son asked her. "Don't you think those kids were just making up their story? Do you think they really saw a UFO?"

"Yes," answered Danuszka. "Because I saw one, too!"

Source: Rzepecki, Bronislaw. "UFOs — A Global Phenomenon." In: Spencer, John, and Hilary Evans, *Phenomenon: From Flying Saucers to UFOs* (London: Futura, 1988), 65–66.

Questions a Ufologist Would Ask:

1. Have you ever had a very vivid dream that seemed real? What was it about?

2. One explanation for some reported encounters with aliens and UFOs is that the experiences were simply very vivid dreams. There is a phenomenon known as sleep paralysis that occurs just as we are about to fall asleep. At that time, we are unable to move our arms or legs but are still slightly awake. If we have a waking dream just as this happens, we may think that we are paralyzed by whatever we are thinking about. This is sometimes used to explain UFO abductions in which people are unable to move when an alien or UFO approaches them.

In the case of Danuszka, it could be said that she simply dreamed the entire experience. However, she did not think she had been dreaming, and she was eventually found in a spot where the others had looked for her. Where was she during that time? Had she been sleepwalking, too?

3. Sometimes we have dreams about ordinary situations, without fantastical things in them like gnomes, monsters, or aliens. If you were having a dream about simply sitting and reading this book, but you thought you were asleep, how could you tell if it was real or imagined?

ARE UFOS REAL?

Do you believe that UFOs are real? Do you think it's possible that aliens have travelled to Earth in spaceships and have been seen by some people?

These are good questions to think about. Although many people say they have seen UFOs and aliens, there is no convincing proof that UFOs are alien spaceships, or that creatures from other planets have visited us. Yet there are thousands of sightings of UFOs reported every year, and there are hundreds of cases on record of people seeing alien beings. And many of the witnesses are children and youth.

While it is fun to wonder about aliens and life elsewhere in the universe, astronomers simply don't know if there are any aliens out there. We have no way of knowing what aliens would look like, how they would act, or what they would say to us.

Could aliens be living somewhere near Earth, and visiting us in spaceships or flying saucers? As far as we know, there are no aliens on other planets in our solar system. Although we have been sending spacecraft such as *Spirit* and *Opportunity* to Mars, the cameras on board have not sent back any video of Martians. There doesn't seem to be any life on Mars, but perhaps other spacecraft will find some hidden somewhere on that planet.

Other planets in our solar system seem to be too hot or too cold to have any life as we know it — Mercury is too close to the sun, and Neptune is too far away.

What about planets around other stars in our galaxy? Could they have alien life? It's possible, but those stars and planets are very, very far away.

How far away? On a typical clear night, you can see about five thousand stars with just your eyes, but those stars are just a fraction of what is actually out there. There are billions and billions of stars in our galaxy, the Milky Way. Astronomers have been able to use telescopes to see distant stars, and some of these have planets. But these are so far away it would take ages to travel here from there.

Imagine that our sun was shrunk down to the size of a pea, sitting on a table in your room. On that scale, the Earth would be completely invisible — much smaller than the point of a pin. But here's the most incredible thing: the next-nearest star, also the size of a pea, would be at least five hundred miles away — on a table in someone else's room, in a different city.

How could we ever travel between stars if they're that far away? It seems so easy on *Star Trek*! Unfortunately, movies and TV shows usually don't present a realistic version of space travel — or at least, they don't present a version that is realistic with current technology. In real life, sending a rocket or space shuttle into space uses tremendous amounts of energy, money, and time. In the coming years, an Earth government will launch a spacecraft to Mars with astronauts aboard. It will take years for the astronauts to make the round trip, and Mars is the nearest planet to Earth. That should give us a small idea of how long and arduous journeys to distant star systems would be.

We don't have the technology or means to make such long, far-reaching voyages — yet. Perhaps in dozens or hundreds of years we will be able to build spacecraft that can carry astronauts safely to a distant planet orbiting a distant star.

But is it possible that aliens on a distant planet have figured out how to do that already? The answer is yes, it is possible. Many planets in our galaxy are much older than Earth, and there may be creatures like us on some of those worlds who are many centuries older than us. They may have developed ways of travelling between stars that we haven't even dreamed of.

If they have, they may have chosen Earth as a place to visit. They may even have parked their huge interstellar spaceship somewhere nearby and have used their flying saucers as "sportscars" to get a closer look at Earth … and of me and you.

But we have no proof that this is really happening. Right now, movies and television shows about such things are simply science fiction. They are stories, and only that.

But they're great stories. And it's even possible that some of the stories in this book are actually true encounters with aliens and UFOs.

If you want more information about UFOs, there are many books to read and websites to browse. Please search for more stories and information; there are even photos and videos available on the Internet that people claim are proof that aliens are here. Some books that you might be able to find about UFOs are given in a reading list later in this book.

HAVE YOU SEEN A UFO?

Do you think you have seen a UFO or alien too? Why not tell us what you saw and send us a drawing of it?

You can send your story and drawing to:

I Saw It Too!
Box 204
Winnipeg, MB, R3V 1L6
Canada

Here are some details that UFO investigators would like to know about what you have seen:

1. Where did you see the UFO? What town or city were you in?
2. What was the month, day, and year?
3. What time did you first see it?

4. What time was it when it was gone? How long did you see it for?

5. Was anyone with you at the time? Did they see it too?

6. What was the shape of the UFO? Did it look like a light in the sky? Was there more than one light together? Was the UFO round? Square? Like a long tube?

7. What colour was it? Did it change colour?

8. Was there a sound?

9. Was it moving? How fast? What direction was it going? Did it change direction?

10. Why do you think this UFO was not simply an airplane, helicopter, star, shooting star, or balloon?

Author's Note: The stories in this book were adapted from actual case histories recorded by UFO investigators and researchers around the world. In some cases, the names of the people who saw the UFOs and aliens have been changed to protect their identities. The locations and dates and times are exactly as given in the original files, however. What the UFOs and aliens looked like and what was said to have happened are also as described by the witnesses, but the actual conversations and what was said by the teenagers, children, and young adults were written for this book, based on what was known about the stories and the people involved.

SUGGESTED READING LIST

Birnes, William. *The UFO Magazine UFO Encyclopedia*. New York: Pocket Books, 2004.

Clark, Jerome. *The UFO Encyclopedia*, Volumes 1–3. Detroit: Apogee Books, 1990.

Curran, Douglas. *In Advance of the Landing: Folk Concepts of Outer Space*. New York: Abbeville Press, 1985.

Dennett, Preston. *UFOs and Aliens (Mysteries, Legends, and Unexplained Phenomena)*. New York: Checkmark Books, 2008.

Elfman, Eric, and Jeff Westover. *Almanac of Alien Encounters*. New York: Random House, 2001.

Herbst, Judith, and Greg Clarke. *The Mystery of UFOs*. New York: Atheneum Press, 1997.

Hynek, J. Allen, and Jacques Vallee. *The Edge of Reality: A Progress Report*. Chicago: Regnery, 1975.

Jacobs, David Michael. *The UFO Controversy in America*. Bloomington, IL: Indiana University Press, 1975.

Klass, Philip J. *UFOs Explained*. New York: Random House, 1974.

Ledger, Don, and Chris Styles. *Dark Object*. Toronto: Dell Publishing, 2001.

Randles, Jenny, and Peter Warrington. *Science and the UFOs*. Oxford, UK: Basil Blackwell, 1985.

Rutkowski, Chris A. *A World of UFOs*. Toronto: Dundurn, 2008.

Ruppelt, Edward J. *The Report of Unidentified Flying Objects*. Garden City, NY: Doubleday, 1956.

Walz-Chojnacki, Greg, and Frank Reddy. *UFOs: True Mysteries or Hoaxes (Isaac Asimov's New Library of the Universe)*. Chicago: Gareth Stevens Publishing, 1995.

ABOUT THE ARTISTS

Stacey May Archer

Stacey was born and raised in Winnipeg, Manitoba. A talented young artist, she is most interested in *anime* and *manga* styles of art and illustration. She enjoys going to concerts and conventions with fellow fans. Stacey has a flair for musical theatre as well; she was "Soupy Sue" in a recent production of the musical *Urinetown* in Winnipeg.

Stacey was recently accepted into graphic design at Red River College in Winnipeg.

Stacey created all the illustrations that accompany the stories in this book, based on her interpretation of the incidents.

Lonigan Gilbert

Lonigan Gilbert is an up-and-coming Van Gogh of this generation, with a life dedicated to his art. He has been good friends with Stacey for years, always sharing his works and helping out.

This is Lonigan's first publication in a book. When he finishes high school he plans to move on to study his one great passion.

He lives in St. Norbert, Manitoba, Canada.